Bulletin No. 46   New Series   June, 1940

FLORIDA FRUITS
AND
VEGETABLES
IN THE
FAMILY MENU

(Reprint)

By
MARY A. STENNIS
Consultant Nutritionist

STATE OF FLORIDA
DEPARTMENT OF AGRICULTURE
Nathan Mayo, Commissioner
TALLAHASSEE

Preface

▼

IN RESPONSE to many requests from within and from without the state, this bulletin has been prepared to acquaint Florida people, and people everywhere, with Florida fruits and vegetables and their nutritive value and uses in the menu.

The great variety of food from which to choose, and the possibilities of food production in the state, are apparent. An increased utilization of Florida's products will come from a better knowledge of their value as a year 'round diet.

NATHAN MAYO,
Commissioner of Agriculture.

Table of Contents

I—Florida's Contribution to the Food Needs of the Nation

FOOD resources tend to concern any section of the country. Transportation and refrigeration have reduced the distribution problem but, even today, an abundant and varied food production is of vital interest. Through science, by means of chemical analyses and animal feeding, we know now that at least 35 simple substances[1] make up man's optimum food supply—that is, the supply necessary to promote normal growth and to maintain health.

We know, too, that of these substances, mineral content is of great importance. Of the ten essential minerals, for instance, calcium and phosphorus must balance each other in proper relation. Sunshine greatly aids not only the plants, but the animals, in the process by which they utilize calcium and phosphorus and thus build good frame structure. Before the sun can do its work, of course, it is essential that the minerals be present—in the soil, in the plant and in the human body. A deficiency of iodine has caused goiter, while a lack of phosphorus in some parts of the world's soil has caused great loss in livestock, the animals becoming bone chewers. Recent research has shown that some copper is necessary in order that the iron may be used for the formation of the red pigment which helps the red corpuscles to carry oxygen to the tissues. The need for lime is recognized as fundamental.

At the present time we feel fairly sure that at least six vitamins are necessary for health. We know, too, that some of these vitamins are water soluble, some are fat soluble, some are in one type of food and missing in others. We have known for a long time that not one protein alone but sixteen digestion products of proteins are needed for body building and that a balance of several foods is required to supply the building food material needed.

Having gone this far, we know that no one food can complete the diet. Variety is essential. Whole wheat bread, for instance, is not vital; cereals for breakfast are not a necessity; but a combination of foods, with a balance of various substances, is essential to optimum health and living. Efforts have been made to prove that the human being can live on milk; can exist on grains; can remain alive on potatoes. Why try to prove possible existence even for a short time? Of what use is bare existence? Abundant life, health, is the goal. Concentrated sugar relieves hunger quickly and so people have believed that sugar has an enormous "food value." It is strictly for energy but, alone, it overtaxes the system. It is habit-forming. It is minus minerals, vitamins, and all structural material for growth and repair. In some sections meat has been published far and wide as the most nearly perfect food and as the most essential food. Meat is a good

[1]Eighteen of these substances are digestive products of proteins; ten are mineral elements (sodium, potassium, calcium, magnesium, chlorine, iodine, phosphorus, sulphur, iron, and copper); six are called vitamins—distinguished as vitamins A, B, C, D, E, and G; one is sugar glucose derived either from glucose or from cane sugar, or starches, milk, sugar, etc.

A GROUP OF VEGETABLES GROWN IN FLORIDA   *Plate Courtesy The Kilgore Seed Company*

protein. It has a limited amount of iron and vitamin G, but it is poor in calcium and has no vitamins other than G.

The normal life history of a human being (or animal) shows that, if born of normal parents, he will start life with vitality, and if well cared for and well fed, will develop a sound body. Some people live well until 80; some die at 40. Some die at 40 and are unburied until 80. They have the privilege of a half life of ill health. Animal feeding has shown that right feeding prolongs life and efficiency and that it affects the rate of growth in the young, the ultimate size, the time for old age to begin to show, the fertility and success of the mothers in raising the young, the reproduction, and the nervous system. The faulty diet of the animal produces physical defects such as short and stocky form, enlarged joints, defective teeth, general runtiness, poor quality of hair, nervousness, abnormal fear—the special symptoms, depending upon the nature of the defect. In addition to this, McCollum and other research authorities tell us that they have seen, repeatedly, each of the deficiency diseases appear in animals deprived of one or another of the required food factors.

Today we still hear, however, that so long as human beings have variety of diet, they are safe. Investigation shows that this is not necessarily true. Wheat, oats, barley, corn, rye, peas, beans, soybeans, potato, sweet potato, radish, turnip, beets, carrot, parsnips, do not supply safety. Add lean meat and yet the safety is not assured. All this list is lacking in the very important item calcium and may be very poor in protein or deficient in vitamins. Leafy vegetables are lacking. Milk is lacking. Both are good sources of calcium. Both are splendid sources of protein. Milk supplies abundant protein while vegetables supply protein in small quantities but of good quality and easily digestible. Fruit is also missing in this list. Fruit, leafy vegetables, and milk are all good sources of vitamins. They should largely supplement even the varied diet above listed.

A cross section of the "Common American Diet of Today" has been pictured for us by a study made by Dr. Lovell Landstrother who made rather true records on the diets of 501 patients suffering from degenerative diseases. Keeping in mind the nation's habit of "meat, bread, potato and dessert" diet, with its usual accessories of butter, cream, sugar, mayonnaise, on the one hand and the so-called "protective" diet (fruit, green vegetables, milk) on the other, he found that 88 per cent of the calories in the total diet was supplied by nonprotective foods and 12 per cent by protective foods. Bread supplied 16 per cent and butter 17 per cent. All except 31 patients used meat; except 107, potato; except 128, sweets; except 36, used vegetables in some amount. Thus 88 per cent were getting a concentrated, too refined and acid diet. Vitamin content was poor, except A which occurred in butter and cream. Carbohydrates was high, calcium low. A protective diet of 70 per cent vegetables, fruit and milk, was prescribed and substituted. The result was that all showed remarkable improvement and 73 per cent recovered.

The diet of the 501 patients studied here is said to be indicative of the American habit of eating. The diseases are in some cases of course, due to heredity, stress of employment, environment, infection, wear and tear, but as was shown in the response of these cases and in thousands of others, partial protection, at least, lies in the "protective" foods—fruits,vegetables and milk.

Our total diet, according to records made by the U. S. Department of Agriculture of over 400 families, includes about 35 per cent wheat flour and 14 per cent sugar. The amount of meat varies and potato comes in for a good share. This "make-up" is poor in vitamins A, C, D, and E, and in calcium and in other minerals. How shall we make up the deficit? Keen competition in placing certain staple foods (as well as "luxuries") on the market has produced confusion and complications in planning the daily menu. Nutritionists who have done the greatest scientific food research have interpreted their findings regarding the essential diet as follows: "A quart of milk will supply about 27 per cent of the total food intake. Two salads—raw— vegetables or fruit each day and a generous serving of green leafy vegetables added to the milk will be a safe plan for health. The appetite will take care of the remainder. A decrease in the milk should mean an increase in fruits and vegetables, always. The solution of the problem lies then in the reduction of sugars and starches, probably meat, and the increase in the protective foods."

What can Florida contribute to the nation's diet, to the happiness, health and efficiency not only of Florida's people but of the nation's population? Does she have a contribution? Does her choice place in the nation, a chosen strip nearest the sun, a selected land with a soil endowed richly with warmth, moisture, calcium, phosphorus and sunshine—a soil receptive to further soil feeding when necessary—have any effect upon her production of "protective" food? Does the fact that Florida receives the purifying effects of the Atlantic breezes from the east and the mild Gulf winds from the west and south, giving her perfect air drainage and a moist atmosphere not of the usual fog and mist of the sea-level type but of a clearness that is seemingly reflected sunlight, mean that the ultra-violet rays of the sun are able to come through more effectively in this favored land?

Tests, made by the Department of Health, Chicago, found that, due to smoke, the ultra-violet rays of the sun were only 50 per cent effective. In tests made in Washington. D. C., with an atmosphere practically free from smoke even the winter sunlight was found effective in successful irradiation. (Anti-rachitic Efficiency of Winter Sunlight of Washington, D. C., Military Surgeon, LXII (1928), 592.) Colonel Brooke in his discussion of "Influence of the Tropics in Rickets" in Annals of Internal Medicine, II (1928), 281, says that the ideal conditions of ultra-violet light are found where the sunlight is most intense and where the atmosphere is free from smoke and cloudiness. Florida is free from smokiness and Florida not only has no long rainy season (as is true in the more tropical locations) but she has very few successive cloudy days during the year.[1] Colonel Brooke also mentions "humidity" as a limiting factor. Does Florida have

---

[1]Average seasonal rainfall in Florida is as follows: winter, 3 inches per month; autumn, 4.39; summer, 6.94; and spring, 3.12.

humidity? She has moisture but very little humidity as the term is commonly used to represent mist and fog.[2] The shifting of the breezes, coming as has been said from the Atlantic on one side and from the Gulf on the other—mild winds of a similarity of temperature—sweeps Florida atmosphere clean and clear, giving her sun free air passage directly to the earth. Even through the season of most rainfall the moisture in the atmosphere precipitates quickly, the atmosphere clears, and the sun "comes through."

Does being nearer the sun mean anything? Florida with a latitude of between 24° 32″ and 31° north, is nearer the sun than is any other state. Dr. Katherine Blunt, University of Chicago, who has recently made a most complete summary of what science knows today of the effect of sunlight on nutrition,[3] says that in the tropics, where the sun's rays are more direct, the intensity of the ultra-violet light is greater, except for cloudiness. Tropical and semi-tropical light has greater anti-rachitic power. she says, and this fact is borne out by the smaller amount of rickets found in such locations. (American Journal of Diseases of Children, XXXV (1928), 590. "Influence of Severe Rickets in New Orleans and Vicinity.")

One other limiting factor remains—that of the sun's altitude, the sun's angle, meaning its distance from the southern horizon, that which makes a difference between summer and winter; between noon, morning or afternoon. Tisdale and Brown ("Relation of the Altitude of the Sun to Its Anti-rachitic Effect," Journal American Medical Association, XCII (March 16, 1929), 860), making tests of the effectiveness of the ultra-violet rays of the sun in the prevention of rickets have reached the conclusion that where the minimal seasonal altitude of the sun is above about 35 degrees the light is protective; and where the sun's altitude is below 35 degrees rickets exist in severe form. The minimal seasonal altitude of the sun at 40 degrees north latitude is 26 degrees; at Glasgow, Scotland, 11 degrees (and below 35 degrees six months); at London, England, 16 degrees (and below 35 degrees for five months); in Boston, 23 degrees (and below 35 degrees for four months); in Baltimore, 27 degrees (below 35 degrees for three months). In Florida the minimum seasonal altitude of the sun is always above 37 degrees, an angle at, or above, which ultra-violet light is always effective.

The three factors limiting the effects of ultra-violet light as stated by Dr. Blunt (namely: the fog, smoke, and dust of the atmosphere, the distance of the sun, and the angle of the sun) having been disposed of satisfactorily, we may, without modification, say that, as far as scientists know, Florida receives more of the effective ultra-violet light of the sun than does any other location in the United States. In simple words we may say Florida occupies the best place in the sun— her vegetables and fruits mature and ripen in the most effective sunshine in the United States.

---

[2]Fog Periods in Florida: Western and extreme north Florida, 12 to 14 days during the year, mostly between November and March; west central coast about 10 days during the year; east coast, less than 10 days; extreme south exceedingly rare, almost never at any time during the year.

[3]"Ultra-Violet Light and Vitamin D in Nutrition" (P. 135), Katherine Blunt.

What does all this sunshine mean? Scientists have, by mechanical means, used ultra-violet rays of light in the treatment of foods and have thereby been able to give certain foods increased health-giving power or what is known as vitamin D. Irradiated foods have shown good results in the better bone building, in the better use of calcium and phosphorus taken into the body. Dr. Katherine Blunt says, "with the limited sunshine of Northern winters, a palatable, readily available food with anti-rachitic power, the power to assist the body in the assimilation of calcium and phosphorus is an important contribution to national health." She refers to irradiated oil treated artificially with this same ultra-violet light which Florida's food products receive from her own natural sunshine, through an almost unobstructed atmosphere, in Nature's own dose, more generous and more effective than that in the northern climate. Is it not at least a more pleasing prospect to take the daily dose, not in oil (artificially treated), but in appetizing, palatable fresh fruit and vegetables?

Since the sun plays such an important part in the process of using the calcium and phosphorus in the human body and has shown some power even in the northern climate to give Vitamin D to a number of foods, including vegetables, cabbage, other greens, soy beans, hay grown in the open in summer, it seems reasonable to conclude that where the light is more effective the storage of vitamins in vegetables and fruits will be greater. Dr. Blunt says that "the scarcity of Vitamin D in northern vegetables may lie partly in the relatively small amount of ultra-violet light in the sunshine and partly in its slight penetrating ability." Various vegetables and orange juice are listed among the foods successfully irradiated. Plants contain the same mother substance, ergosterol,[1] upon which light acts in human cells to produce Vitamin D. Therefore if the sunlight in the proper intensity and at the proper angle can reach the plant for a sufficient period, it is reasonable to believe that the same good work proceeds— the storing of Vitamin D for human use. Florida, having the year 'round advantage of all other locations in the United States in the quality of her sunshine, furnishes a field for unlimited research along these lines.

Artificial irradiation has been found to be effective, if properly used, but harmfully so, if overdone. Irradiated ergosterol[2] (Viosterol) has been successfully used but also misused. The United States Public Health Service says, "Of course we would not be understood as deprecating the therapeutic use of irradiated ergosterol, but would rather call attention to the possible harm that might result from too large doses." Foods over-irradiated have been found to be ineffective.

---

[1]Ergosterol, the parent substance of vitamin D, is a sterol found always wherever cholesterol occurs. It exists in largest quantities in ergot or in yeast. Phylesterol, too— the sterol common in plants—is accompanied by ergosterol. Irradiated ergosterol, even a one per cent solution in oil, is very potent, two and a half to ten drops being equivalent to one cup of good grade cod liver oil.

[2]Viosterol, the new standard product of irradiated ergosterol, is much less concentrated than the above-mentioned irradiated ergosterol, a dose of eight to ten drops being equivalent to three to five teaspoons of cod liver oil. "Ultra-Violet Light and Vitamin D in Nutrition," Katherine Blunt.

Equipment for artificial irradiation has been found to be not yet dependable. There is much that is uncertain. There is a broad field of research open for future scientists. But, in the light of what has been done, there is the satisfaction that in Florida sunlight at least, if we make full use of the sun food products—fruits and vegetables —there is reason to believe protective power does exist.

Sunlight, however, is not the whole story. Fruits and vegetables come from the soil. Plant food must come from the soil. Again calcium and phosphorus are essential. Florida soil, in many sections, abounds in lime. Calcium and phosphorus exist in vast stores. In fact, Florida produces more phosphate than any other state in the Union. These two minerals, among others, are available within the state. Florida's soils by experiment have shown that they are easily receptive to such additional mineral food as is needed. By soil selection and by proper supplementary feeding all the vegetables and fruits of the warm climate type and many of the temperate climate type may be produced economically and successfully, and well stored with the calcium, phosphorus and other minerals necessary in animal and human nutrition.

From January to January throughout the entire breadth and length of the state from Pensacola to Key West, fruits and vegetables of some type or of many types are "in season" and not only in season but in sunshine. Not only are they in sunshine but out-of-doors in sunshine, fully exposed and nautral in their development, and in a soil so varied and adaptable that suitable plant feeding locations are easily available for a big variety of the known fruits and vegetables and for many varieties not known elsewhere. With an abundant and effective sunshine all year, a generous moisture, a soil containing mineral food[1] and receptive to added mineral foods, Florida, an all-'round, all-year agricultural possibility, has a wealth of health not only for herself but for the country at large to whom she sends her luscious fruits and fresh nutritious vegetables. The minerals, vitamins and roughage she sends abroad are adding to the nation's wealth, health and efficiency. From the modest little red-haw or blueberry of northwest Florida, over the wide range of hundreds of fruits to the gorgeous mango of the far south; from the "first families" of the "greens" of north Florida to the newly-rich romaine of the south there is reason to believe that these food plants have gleaned, in the growing, the best Nature has to offer.

---

[1] "Soils of Florida," O. C. Bryan, published by the Florida State Department of Agriculture.

II—Florida Vegetables

WHY MORE VEGETABLES? GREEN, FRESH, VEGETABLES?

VEGETABLES, next to milk—particularly the green, leafy vegetables—supply the body with more mineral food than does any other class of foods. "An edible leaf," McCollum tells us, "is essentially a complete and nearly or quite balanced food." Animals have subsisted for generations on the leaves of plants. Animals do not succeed on grain, tuber, or root diet. Hogs fed largely on peanuts and sweet potatoes have a soft oily fat and fragile bones. As hay and forage go into the diet of the animals, the leafy green should enter the human diet.

Protective Value

Vegetables are rich in calcium. All other foods except milk are poor in calcium. Calcium is absolutely essential for body building. It must come from the soil to the plant to the human body for proper nutrition. Leaf vegetables are also rich in other necessary minerals as are also root vegetables. They supplement each other. But the leafy fresh vegetable goes further than other foods—grains, tubers, roots, meat or even fruit—in furnishing the minerals and thus keeps the body in the proper neutral or very slightly alkaline condition.

Vegetables have a vitamin content which supplements that of cereals, roots, and tubers and even fruits. Here again the green leafy vegetables and the yellow types excel.

Vegetables have a contribution to make in protein—small but very valuable in that it again supplements cereals. In fact the protein of the green leaf helps the body to utilize the protein of cereals.

Mechanical Value

In addition to the regulation effected by the minerals contained in vegetables there is a very definite aid rendered to the mechanical process of digestion. Vegetables possess an amount of non-digestible matter of water holding capacity and are thus able to maintain a favorable consistency for elimination. The so-called "roughage" of vegetables is non-irritating to the delicate linings of the alimentary tract. The starchy roots also make a contribution in "non-digestibles" capable of swelling in water.

FLORIDA VEGETABLES AVAILABLE FOR HOME USE

JERUSALEM ARTICHOKE

Jerusalem artichoke is an underground tuber of the sunflower family. It is not an artichoke and it is not from Jerusalem. It is native to the United States and was used among the early Indians.

The tubers are elongated to round in shape. They are red and yellow to white in color, the flesh being white. The skin is rough, with many eyes, the general appearance being that of a potato.

The composition of this tuber is different from that of the potato, being about 14.7 per cent sugar and 0 per cent starch. It is an agreeable change from potato and it may be cooked in a similar manner.

ASPARAGUS

Asparagus is 94 per cent water, but the edible portion contains more protein than most succulent vegetables. Its delicate flavor, its quick growth and tender quality, its ready digestibility, make it popular in Florida where it appears in what is still winter elsewhere.

The tender, young, white or greenish-white stems of asparagus are used as food. Preparatory to cooking, cut off the woody base or snap off the stems with a sharp knife. Tie the stems in neat bundles and place them in boiling salted water for 20 minutes with the cut ends resting on the bottom of the vessel; then drop on sides so that the heads will be submerged, and cook until tender. Serve with warm butter, or on well-toasted bread, and season with pepper and salt.

LIMA BEANS

Limas are kidney shaped flat beans. They grow well even in the hot summer. They should be used the day they are picked if desired fresh. Use soft water for cooking or else the lime of the hard water forms an insoluble compound with the protein of the bean. Combined with sweet green corn they make a favorite well-known Indian dish known as succotash, usually made by cooking the green beans from twenty to thirty minutes and combining them with canned corn. The mixture is then tossed into a pan containing finely chopped fried hot bacon or is seasoned with butter.

GREEN STRING BEANS

Green beans have shown at least as much vitamin A as head lettuce and much more than the inner leaves of fresh cabbage. They are particularly rich in vitamin C when fresh. String beans grown in Florida have a texture more tender and a flavor more delicate than beans in climates of slower growth. They are similar to "greens" in food value when young and tender. To prepare for cooking break off and discard the ends of the pods; break into pieces, wash well and drop into boiling water and cook rapidly for fifteen minutes. Allow water to evaporate. Season well with salt and butter or with bacon. Place over a slow heat and cook 30 minutes longer. Do not "soak" beans before cooking. This process loses flavor and food value. Sometimes a distinction is made between string beans and snap beans, the latter being smaller but similar in food value and method of preparation. (Bulletin 23, Florida State Department of Agriculture.)

BEETS

Greens—Beet greens contain vitamin A and are rich in calcium. They are somewhat like chard. When young the entire plant, including the root, may be used as "greens." Wash thoroughly and cook from 20 to 30 minutes in boiling salted water. Chop in fine pieces. Season with butter and cream. Serve hot.

Roots—The roots of beets supply some iron and phosphorus and have a small vitamin C content. Beets contain a certain amount of sugar and starch but very little protein. They add attractiveness of color. Beets lose much of their nutritive material and color in cooking and should be cooked in the skins and with at least two inches of the top. Boil for one hour in a large volume of water. Leave the lid on. For a quick method peel and slice or chop finely. Add a very small amount of

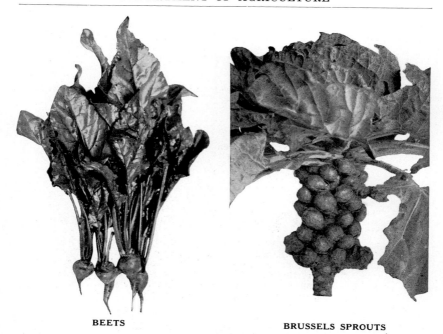

BEETS   BRUSSELS SPROUTS

water and cook for 15 minutes. Add lemon juice and butter. Serve hot. Beets adapt themselves nicely to waterless cookers. Put unpeeled beets in a saucepan with three tablespoons water. Cook until tender. Peel and dress with butter, pepper and salt. They are sweeter and of better flavor cooked by this method. A sauce of one tablespoon vinegar, 2 tablespoons butter, ½ teaspoon scraped onion, one tablespoon sugar and ½ teaspoon of salt may be made to give small beets a piquant flavor. Pour over peeled beets and let stand in a covered hot pan a few minutes.

BROCCOLI

Broccoli is a winter vegetable in Florida. It looks a little like the cauliflower but is more hardy. It contains probably more vitamin A than cauliflower but otherwise is similar in composition. Select when young and tender.

BRUSSELS SPROUTS

Brussels sprouts is a variety of cabbage, having blistered leaves and the stem of the plant covered with small heads of cabbage which form the edible portion of the plant, and which are more delicate in flavor than the cauliflower or cabbage. It is used as cabbage in the menu. It contains more vitamin A than the white leaves of cabbage.

BREADFRUIT

The breadfruit tree (40 feet high) resembles a big chestnut tree. Breadfruit is oval shaped something like a melon. It is covered with short, hard projections. The skin is green and is marked in small hexagons. The stem should be cut and covered with salt and the fruit kept until it turns brown. The fruit has a considerable amount of starch and a higher caloric value than the banana. The ash fiber and protein are high. It is a good source of vitamin A but has no B or C.

To prepare, put in the oven and bake. When cooked, open and season with butter, pepper and salt. Fresh breadfruit may be cut in slices and dried in the sun. A paste called "Mahe" is sometimes made. This ferments and has a disagreeable odor but when cooked the paste is a good nutritious food. The sago-like farinaceous pellets inside are often made into puddings.

JACKFRUIT

The jackfruit is the largest of tropical fruits, being sometimes two feet long and weighing forty pounds. It grows from the trunk of the tree. It has a hard rind which has to be cut with an axe. It is green, then greenish-yellow and finally brown as it ripens. Inside are numerous small cavities each with a seed surrounded by a soft brownish pulp, somewhat suggestive of banana. It is eaten fresh or preserved. When the flesh is boiled in fresh milk and strained off, the milk, when cold, becomes a gelatinous consistency of blanc-mange of orange color and melon flavor. The seeds boiled or roasted are good to eat.

CABBAGE

This plant probably ascended from the "colwart" or collard. It stands high as a "protective" food due to its high vitamin content of A, B and C, and to its generous supply of calcium. It loses some vitamin C in cooking. The flavor and

KILGORE'S WAKEFIELD CABBAGE

digestibility of the raw material seem to rate higher than that of the cooked product. Cabbage and other members of the cabbage family have some sulphur compounds which when boiled in water produce a disagreeable odor and the volatile substance given off in the steam is disagreeable. The container should be left open for a few minutes at least. Young tender cabbage may be steamed. It is delicious when cooked in the water where a ham bone has been boiled. Raw cabbage lends itself to many varieties of dishes and combinations. (See Salads.) (Bulletin **23**, Florida State Department of Agriculture.)

OTHER CABBAGES

1. Chinese Cabbage (Pe-tsai)—This cabbage is made of white, close-growing stems with green leaves. The centers are very tender and may be used for raw salads. To cook, cut and place in boiling salted water for **30** minutes or less. Season with butter and lemon juice.

2. Cauliflower—Cauliflower and broccoli are about the only flowers used as vegetables. Cauliflower is considered as a cabbage, but it is milder in flavor and possibly more easily digested. It has a high water holding capacity. It is a good source of calcium, having nearly twice as much as any other vegetable. It is expensive.

The principle of cooking is the same as for cabbage. Soak it upside down in salt (mild) water to kill insects hiding there. (Bulletin **23**, Florida State Department of Agriculture.)

3. Rape—Rape, sometimes called Portuguese Cabbage, is used in the very young tender stage for greens. It is cooked in boiling water about **30** minutes. Grated cocoanut or tomato catsup make a good seasoning.

IMPROVED PEKIN CELERY CABBAGE

4. Kohl-Rabi—Kohl-Rabi has from one to three times as much phosphorus, calcium, and protein as have beets and carrots—it also has as much iron.

Kohl-Rabi or turnip cabbage has the stem or bulb, the edible portion of the plant, largely above the ground. The smaller bulbs are less tough and fibrous than the larger ones. To prepare, cut the leaves and bulbs in small pieces. Boil the bulb in salted water 15 minutes. Then add the leaves and cook another 30 minutes. Slice the bulbs. Arrange the greens around the edge of the plate and the bulb slices in the center. Use melted butter.

CARROT

The carrot, rich in an essential oil that gives it a strong odor or flavor, sometimes objectionable, has, on the other hand, a yellow pigment (tasteless and odorless) that gives it a beautiful color always desirable in planning a menu.

Carrots are about 12 per cent solid matter, about half of which is sugar. The outer layer contains pectin. Young carrots possess greater caloric value than old carrots, the latter having a tendency to become woody.

Calcium and vitamins A, B and C are well stored in carrots. The indigestible carbohydrates, pectin, etc., are a mechanical aid in digestion and elimination. Recent experiments show that the peel contains more vitamin B than the flesh. Grated, young, raw carrots easily include the peel and are more attractive in flavor than the cooked product. Because of the rich coloring and the pectin content, carrots are combined with pineapple and some other fruits, lacking in pectin, in the making of marmalades. (Bulletin 23, Florida State Department of Agriculture.)

CASSAVA (S.)

Cassava is a starchy root or underground stem. There are two kinds, bitter and sweet. The plant is 4 to 6 feet high. The roots containing the starch sometimes grow to be 4 feet long and about 2 inches in diameter. These roots are of pure white solid tissue harder and drier than potato. They have a reddish bark easily removed. The sweet varieties the natives in the tropics peel and cook. They make a thin cake from the meal. It is "Cassava bread." McCollum tells us that cassava and other tropical roots contain ergosterol which after it has been taken into the body becomes activated by the ultra-violet light of the nearby sun. Thus vitamin D is produced. (Bulletin 31, Florida State Department of Agriculture.)

CELERY

Celery is a winter crop in Florida where, on fewer acres, more celery is produced than in any other state. The enlarged succulent stalk of the basal leaves is the edible portion. Celery salt is ground celery seed and is highly prized for flavoring soups and salads. Celery leaves (green) have vitamin A, the stalks have some A and are good in vitamin B. A very small quantity of essential oil gives celery its taste. Celery may nearly always be obtained even when other fresh vegetables are scarce. It often gives variety to an otherwise "soft" and concentrated menu. Since this is true it should really not be cooked except as a flavor and then only slightly cooked so that it will afford a good "crunchy feel" and something to chew, something with which to give the teeth proper exercise. The outside leaves and tougher portions may be used in soups, sauces, stews, omelets or cooked dressings. (Volume 36, No. 2, Florida State Department of Agriculture, "Celery Growing in Florida.")

SWISS CHARD   CELERY

SWISS CHARD

Swiss chard, a variety of beet which, instead of a root, has thick, broad leaves growing on a large succulent stem. The outside leaves may be removed and used and the plant left to grow. Chard is a good source of vitamin A and calcium. It should be cooked in a small amount of water. Stir until the leaves settle in the water.

SWEET CORN

Corn is a cereal, but in its fresh green state deserves mention in this list. To prepare, place in boiling salted water for 10-12 minutes. Serve hot with butter. Be careful not to overcook. Yellow corn probably is a richer source of vitamin A than is white corn.

COLLARDS

Collards belong to the non-heading thick-leaf vegetables growing on one stalk. Both cooked and raw they are excellent in vitamin A. They are also a source of vitamins B and C. They are a good winter vegetable and are improved with cool mornings and light frosts. In colder climates the leaves form loose heads but in Florida they do not head. Leaves may be broken from the stems and the plant left to continue to grow through the winter.

CUCUMBER

The cucumber is about 96 per cent water. It lends freshness and crispness to the meal. It grows very rapidly in Florida, is tender and appetizing even when large in size. Fresh in salads is the best form of preparation. It may be brined, then treated with boiling vinegar with or without sugar or spices. "Dill pickles" are usually large cucumbers flavored with dill seeds. As an appetizer to vary a diet, cucumbers supply a cool, palatable relish. To cook, peel, slice in quarters lengthwise and put into boiling water and boil five minutes, or steam. Season with butter, pepper, and salt. Turn heat low, cover closely. Cook 30 minutes. A prickly variety, small in size, is the Gherkin, particularly good for pickling. (Bulletin 23, Florida State Department of Agriculture.)

ENDIVE

This plant has a greenish-white stem with a rosette of curly light-green leaves which make an attractive garnish for salads or cooked dish—the curly type for salads, and the broad-leaf type for cooking. It has a bitter flavor which some call a "tonic." The bleached leaves are more crisp and tender. It is best served with a French dressing of oil and lemon juice. Sometimes a bit of hot bacon grease, instead of oil, is added to the lemon juice for seasoning.

EGG PLANT

Egg plant has a low food value. It may be fried, baked or steamed. It adds bulk, variety and interest to the diet. It forms a good basis for combination foods.

GARLIC

Garlic resembles onion sets in appearance but has a white papery outer shell. Remove the outer covering and slice through. It is very strong in flavor. **Use very sparingly.**

LETTUCE

FLORIDA HEAD LETTUCE

Lettuce is particularly known for its vitamin, the **green** raw leaves being excellent in A and C and good in B and E. Its mineral salts are abundant. Some people have thought that lettuce has a medicinal virtue due to a small quantity of sleep inducing substance called lactucarium. This is found more in the stem, however. Others have thought that the iron is particularly valuable in that it is in original form, chemically confined in the chlorophyl. Lettuce does not have as much iron as spinach and turnip greens. It lends itself most agreeably to the making of salads. It is usually eaten raw and is therefore not depleted in food value.

ESCAROLE

Escarole is a large non-heading curly lettuce growing on one stalk. It is listed as excellent in vitamin A and is of a rich green color. The outer as well as the inner

ESCAROLE

leaves should be eaten. To prepare for salad chill thoroughly. Another way of serving is to tie the outer leaves together and drop them into hot soup for 5 minutes. Remove the lettuce, taking care to retain its shape, and squeeze dry. Cut in inch lengths and serve hot, capped with grated cheese, or chop fine and serve with melted butter and a little cream. Non-heading lettuce is delicious served wilted with bacon, or cooked as "greens."

WATER CRESS

Water cress consists of long tender stems having small lobed leaves. It is used in salads or cooked like "greens." It is an excellent source of vitamins A and C. It should be grown in good water—water that is fit to drink. Para cress grows in extreme south Florida and is known as toothache plant. It presumably has some narcotic quality. It is used in salads.

Recent research made by Mendel and Vickery Laboratory Physiological Chemistry, finds water cress leaves notably "rich in vitamin A; comparable with other vegetables in dietary factors formerly called vitamin B; more potent than lettuce in vitamin E." (Jour. Home Economics, July, 1930.)

MINT

Mint consists of small green leaves with an aromatic flavor. It may be chopped fine or used whole to flavor fruit cocktails, salads or jelly. It is convenient to make a mint sauce by mixing it with sugar and vinegar or with sugar and lemon juice. It sometimes is used with peas and new potatoes and to flavor chutney and preserves.

MINT

GREEN MUSTARD

Mustard has green crumpled leaves which should be crisp and a vivid green. To prepare, cut crosswise finely and boil in a little water for five minutes. Season with butter, salt and pepper. Cover and cook slowly 30 minutes.

CHINESE MUSTARD

The Chinese mustard is a hot weather green whereas the common mustard is of agreeable flavor only in cool weather. The Chinese variety has a half pungent flavor very agreeable.

KALE

This is a quick growing thick leaf green plant, rich in vitamin A.

DANDELION

The thick-leaved, large-leaved variety will grow in Florida but has not been used to any great extent. It is used in salads and in cooking.

OKRA

The okra plant is similar to the cotton plant. It is a dry weather fruiting plant and thrives through the hot, dry season when other vegetables are scarce. It grows easily nearly all over the state and bears well over a period of several weeks.

The fruit is a small green pod and is best selected when young and tender. It has a vitamin B content. The flavor is most pleasing in soups. The mucilaginous consistency is a means of thickening soup. The texture of full grown okra is to some palates not agreeable but if the pods are selected early and lightly boiled or steamed so as not to break the skins the effect is good and usually successful. Okra with tomatoes (gumbo) is a delightful dish, the tomato lending the acid flavor and the okra thickening the tomato to a pleasing consistency. (Bulletin 23, Florida State Department of Agriculture.)

ONION

Onions, raw, are good sources of vitamin C. Onions have been ranked with oranges, lemons, tomatoes and raw cabbage in richness in vitamin C. Osborne and Mendel rank onions with about the same vegetables and fruits as source of vitamin B. Onions contain from 10 to 15 per cent nutrients. Bermudas, shallots and leeks and other green onions grow abundantly in Florida. The mineral value and the "nerve tonic" idea have probably been over-rated but there seems to be no doubt about the laxative effect of onions. They are classed as thick-leaf vegetables.

Green Onion

Green or immature onions are long, slender, white stalks having tubular green leaves. To prepare for the table, remove the green tops, and serve raw as a relish in salad, or chop and use in stews or "combination" dishes.

Mature Onion

The Spanish or Bermuda onion is a spherical-shaped or flattened bulb having a dead, shriveled stem and a dry, tan-colored, papery outer husk. To prepare for the table, peel from the root up, place in rapidly boiling water and cook for 5 minutes. Let the water evaporate, and season the vegetable with butter, salt and pepper. Cover closely and steam for 30 minutes. To bake, place for 5 minutes in rapidly boiling salted water, then remove, and put under meat to be roasted. (Selected.) (Extension Bulletin 9, Hawaii Experiment Station.)

Pickling Onion

Pickling or Portuguese onions are small, round, partly mature bulbs which are sold in bunches. Owing to their flavor, they are especially fine for pickling whole in vinegar, or for use in stews and salads. To pickle, select very fresh onions and peel them from the root up, taking care to keep the bulb whole and round. While peeling, drop into a salt solution made by dissolving 2 tablespoons of salt in 2 cups of cold water to prevent discoloration and softening. When ready to pickle (this may be done immediately if desired), dry on a cheesecloth and drop into a hot ster-ilized bottle, adding boiling hot vinegar to cover. To prepare the vinegar for 4 pounds of small onions, boil 2 cups of malt vinegar with 1 tablespoon of salt, 1 dozen peppercorns, 6 allspices, 3 bay leaves, and 6 small red peppers. Seal the bottled onions and keep them in a dark place. (Selected.) (Extension Bulletin 9, Hawaii Experiment Station.)

CHIVES

Chives are milder and more tender than onions. They are grown for the leaves and are useful in salads, soups, and stews.

SHALLOT

Shallots are small clustered bulbs which resemble partly mature pickling onions.

but have fine, slender leaves. To cook, remove the tops and steam the bulbs. Serve with butter. The delicate nutty flavor of shallots is very pleasing.

PARSLEY

Parsley consists of sprays of bright green, finely curled dissected leaves. It is used for soups, stews, sauces and to garnish salads, or cooked vegetables. It gives attractive color.

PARSNIPS

The parsnip is a winter vegetable. It has more starch, more sugar than the carrot and turnip. It also has a generous amount of pectin and cellulose. To prepare, peel thickly, cook one hour in water to cover. Mash and season with milk, pepper and salt, or mash with finely chopped browned bacon.

PEAS

Peas and beans are used as food both in the green and in the dry stage. They have a high protein content. In the dry stage they contain a high percentage of protein but do not take the place of meat due to the fact that the proteins of legumes are not the only proteins needed in body building and repair. These vegetables also furnish a fair amount of iron and phosphorus and some calcium. They, although high in protein, are alkaline in reaction. Fresh green peas or fresh cowpeas have good supply of vitamins A, B and C. Dried leaves and peas may be counted upon for vitamin B. Green peas (English peas) are a winter crop in Florida while the cowpeas, lady-peas and black-eyed peas flourish during the summer season.

The field pea is a Southern dish. Experiments made by the U. S. Department of Agriculture (Farmer's Bulletin 318) as to the nutritional value of the field pea shows that it compares favorably with other legumes. Long and general use on Southern tables proves its satisfactory food value. The lady-pea was found more digestible than the kidney bean, 83 per cent of the protein and 95 per cent of the carbohydrates being digested. The sugar crowder and lady are popular. The bush conch is a popular Florida table pea. (Bulletin 23, Florida State Department of Agriculture.)

PIGEON PEA (S.)

This pea grows on a tall, woody, half-hardy shrub that yields heavily. The unripe pea is used for the English pea and has been pronounced a good starting point for a tropical green pea.

"RED" PEPPER

Red peppers or long "hot" peppers are tapering pods which are first green, then red when matured. They are used in pickles, chutney, sauces, for seasoning. The juice is very strong and should be used **sparingly.** These peppers are easily cured or dried in the sun.

SWEET PEPPERS

Sweet peppers in Florida sometimes bear as long as 6 or 8 months in the year. **Pimentos** are smooth, have a thick, juicy flesh and are sweeter than the other types. They are better for canning. Tests of canned pimentos made by MacLeod, Nutrition Laboratory, Columbia (Journal Home Economics, July, 1930), showed a vitamin C content equal to that of grapefruit.

The **bell pepper** is hardier than the pimento but has a good flavor and color. "Stuffed peppers" is a favorite Southern dish. Peppers for salads should be well crisped. Peppers for canning should be placed in a hot (not warm) oven for loosening the peel. (Bulletin 23, page 29, Florida State Department of Agriculture.)

POTATOES

The potato is a modified stem, an enlargement for storing starch. It shows in an analysis some potash, a small amount of iron, calcium, and phosphorus. Both white and sweet potatoes show vitamin C content and the sweet potato (the yellow variety) shows a greater vitamin A content. Both potatoes contain very little cellulose. They yield an alkaline ash and are cheap sources of vitamin C which occurs more often in the "luxuries." They help to balance the acid residue of meat.

White Potato

Very young potatoes and old potatoes (ready to sprout) have less starch and more sugar than well grown but still fresh potatoes. The average potato (mature) has 75 per cent water, 20 per cent starch, and about one-eighth that much protein, and a relatively large amount of ash as compared with other vegetables. The more moist potatoes have a greater proportion of protein while the mealy potato has more starch. Experimental cooking of the potato has shown that in boiling (peeled) 8.2 per cent of the protein is lost when the potatoes are plunged directly into boiling water, 25 per cent when they are soaked beforehand, and 15.8 per cent when they are placed in cold water and brought to a boil. When boiled in the jackets they lose only one per cent of the protein and only three per cent of the mineral. Baking potatoes loses almost none of the nutrients. (Bulletin No. 3, Florida State Department of Agriculture.)

Sweet Potato

Many varieties of sweet potato flourish in Florida soils. Usually the moist sweeter potato goes on the local market while the dry mealy article is sent to the Northerner who likes it better. The sweet variety has from 6 to 8 per cent sugar and therefore a higher caloric value than the white potato. The sugar increases while the starch decreases during storage. The protein percentage is possibly a little less in the sweet potato. Peanuts are a splendid supplement and are combined in many interesting ways with the sweet potato. (See Recipes.)

Canning factories are now taking care of the small potatoes not suitable for shipping and are supplying localities not able to purchase the fresh potato all year. Recently canneries in Florida have begun also to can the white potato too small to ship. Now a vegetable dinner with potato is being placed in one can for the market.

The "Porto Rico," rich in color, moist in texture, sweet in flavor, and the Nancy Hall, with a creamy pink yellow flesh, are two of the more popular varieties among Southern people. The Triumph and Big Stem Jersey, dry and mealy in texture, are more popular among Northern people who are more accustomed to the white potato and who like the drier type. Various yam varieties are splendid for home use but are rather tender and easily bruised in handling. (Bulletin 31, Florida State Department of Agriculture.)

YAM

This is not a sweet potato. It is a larger tuber than the sweet potato and not so sweet. When it grows to unusual size it is tougher and coarser than the sweet potato. It keeps more easily than the potato. In the lower part of the state it remains in the ground from year to year without replanting. Negroes use it for bread. They "dig" it as they need it from day to day.

DASHEEN

The dasheen is an underground corm or tuber in which the plant stores starch. The leaves are similar to "Elephant Ear." It is similar to the white potato but has less water and more starch and protein. It has a nutty flavor when cooked by boiling or baking, that suggests boiled chestnuts. It is served with drawn butter. It bakes nicely. The dasheen makes a successful fluted "crisp" to be eaten with the fingers like potato chips. Dasheen leaves are also used as greens. They should be selected when young and tender. (Bulletin 31, Florida State Department of Agriculture.)

PLANTAIN
(Cooking Banana)

Plantain has the appearance of a very large coarse banana. It is not edible raw but is a good source of vitamins A and B in the cooked stage. It should be cooked slowly. Before it is ripe it may be sliced very thin and cooked like potato chips. It may also be baked or boiled. It is akin to the sweet potato in taste and texture when cooked. Lemon juice and butter add to the flavor.

RADISH

Radish greens are the tops of the little radish roots and are suitable to combine with other varieties of spring or winter "greens." The roots are peppery in flavor, attractive for salads, and are easily and quickly grown in early spring. Radishes are a source of vitamins B and C and the greens carry A.

SALSIFY

Salsify or oyster plant consists of long brown roots. It grows wild or may be cultivated. To prepare, scrape and cut into one-inch pieces. Drop into boiling water and let boil 5 minutes; then place in a creamy white sauce and boil 30 minutes. To fry cut in 2- or 3-inch lengths, dip in flavor, then in egg and crumbs and fry in deep fat. The food has a delicate flavor which suggests oysters. Select young.

SPINACH

Spinach has slender, succulent stems having small leaves. It has a highly alkaline residue in the process of digestion. It is rich in iron and in vitamins A, B and C. According to Sherman it has as much vitamin A as an equal weight of egg yolk or butter. It needs only a few minutes high temperature in cooking and therefore maintains its rich vitamin content. It is better steamed than boiled. Lemon juice helps the flavor. Add butter. Serve hot.

NEW ZEALAND SPINACH

This vegetable is not related to the ordinary spinach. It is a hot weather grower and forms a good substitute for spinach during the season when spinach does not thrive. It is cooked as "greens" and is popular often among people who do not like spinach.

NEW ZEALAND SPINACH

SQUASH

1. Winter Squash — Winter squash may be seeded and peeled thinly and steamed, mashed and served with butter, salt and pepper. Or it may be steamed in slices for serving. By placing a towel on the steamer rack, the squash on the towel, and another cloth over the food, the extra moisture is absorbed and the squash is a nice, tender consistency, yet firm and not "watery."

2. Chinese Squash — Chinese squash or melon is a light green color. It has a whitish, fuzzy appearance when young. It is round or slightly elongated. The rind is like a watermelon. The meat, about 2 inches thick, is white, as are also the seed. The flavor is mild. It forms a good casserole lining for squab or chicken.

3. Hubbard Squash—Hubbard squash or pumpkin is oval-shaped, greenish-yellow and has a good amount of vitamin A. Without removing the peel place in the oven and bake slowly 45 minutes. Cut into neat pieces. Serve in the skin.

4. Summer Squash—Summer squash is a light green, oval shape. Serve like Chinese squash. Yellow squash is said to have more vitamin A than the white variety. (Bulletin 23, Florida State Department of Agriculture.)

5. Chayote—The chayote grows on a climbing vine. The fruit is pear-shaped more or less and varies in size and color as well as shape. It has one big seed. Like squash, and is better cut into slices for serving and steamed only until tender. Chayote in the raw state has only a fair amount of vitamin A and seemingly no vitamin B or C.

To prepare for cooking, peel, slice or dice. This squash may be creamed, fried in butter, made into fritters, salads or pickles. A sauce may be made by boiling or steaming and mashing the fruit and adding the juice of the flowers of the roselle (a beautiful red). When sugar is added a good dessert is the result.

The chayote will thrive when other vegetables are usually scarce. When once established it continues to grow year after year.

TOMATO

The tomato is in season in some localities almost the year 'round in Florida. It is one of the most common, yet most valuable, of Florida vegetables. It is the vegetable richest in vitamins, particularly vitamin C, the one most lacking in the American diet. Tomato juice should be a part of the diet of everybody, beginning with the babies only a few weeks of age. Orange juice and tomato juice, easily taken, are splendid supplements of deficient diets. They are "fool proof" in nutritional value. Fresh or canned tomatoes add variety, color, food value (both mineral and vitamin), flavor, and pleasure to any menu. (Bulletin **23**, State Department of Agriculture.)

PLUM TOMATO

The plum tomato is a small oval-shaped tomato varying from yellow to red. It is good for cooking purposes, particularly for preserves.

TURNIPS

Turnip greens are the tops of the common turnip. They are usually rich in iron and calcium. They are a valuable source of vitamins A, B and C. They should be selected young and tender and cooked quickly. The liquor in which they are cooked should be used for soups. Bacon adds a splendid flavor to turnip greens. These greens are not easily hurt by frost and light freezes. They are hardy and should be grown all winter.

TURNIPS

Root turnips are good in vitamins B and C and the yellow turnips probably contain vitamin A. They have a spicy, pungent taste (due to an essential oil) and, when combined with the turnip greens and slices of cured bacon and hot corn muffins, they form a favorite **fall** meal in the South. It is said that the juices of tomatoes and turnip greens have had a big place in the list of protective foods in the southern climate. (Bulletin **31**, Florida State Department of Agriculture.)

Swedish Turnip (Rutabaga)— The rutabaga has a denser yellow flesh and takes longer to mature than the white turnip. The roots can stand longer summer heat without becoming woody or acrid. The yellow turnip surpasses the white in its vitamin A content and it also contains more sugar.

III—Florida Fruits

WHY MORE FRUITS? FRESH FRUITS?

FRUITS have a very decided nutritive value. Although people, in some climates, consider fruit a mere luxury, it is well known that in tropical climates many natives practically live on fruits. Many people, on the other hand, use fruit as a medicine due largely to its hygienic value rather than to its food value. According to Farmers Bulletin No. 293, U. S. Department of Agriculture, a study of the diets of 400 families in the United States showed that 4.4 per cent of the total food material and 3.7 per cent of the total carbohydrates used are from fruit. As to digestibility, it is estimated that 80 per cent of the protein, 97 per cent of the fat, and 95 per cent of the carbohydrates in fruits are digested. It is not the purpose of this bulletin to compare a vegetable diet with a meat diet but in the light of various experiment station records it seems safe to say that a fruit and nut diet, plus a liberal amount of cereal and vegetables and eggs with a limited amount of meat, makes a more attractive variety of adequate food of less bulk and of less cost than does the usual meat, potato and sugar diet.

A wise use of fruit is certainly beneficial if the particular needs of the system are considered. The organic acids of the fruit, which increase the flow of saliva and indirectly of gastric juice, aid digestion. These acids increase the secretions of the liver, pancreas, and of the mucous linings of the intestines. They serve, also, to keep the upper intestinal contents free from harmful bacteria. Fruits help to keep the fluids and tissues of the body in neutral or slightly alkaline condition by supplying minerals, especially calcium, phosphorus and iron and in this way they help to overcome the acid reaction of the meat, egg and starch foods. Vitamins, particularly vitamin C (usually absent in foods other than fresh fruits such as citrus, tomatoes and fresh uncooked leaves and very important in the building and preservation of teeth) are generously supplied. An appetite is stimulated both by the vitamins in fresh fruit and by the attractive flavor and appearance.

Ripe fruit, poor in protein, furnishes a small proportion of building and energy foods. A very large and expensive amount of fruit would be necessary to furnish as much protein as a small package of peas, beans or cereals. Nevertheless, fruits are necessary and should be used regularly.

From the standpoint of calories (energy value), ripe fruits supply mainly sugar. In nearly all fruits the ripening process changes starch to sugar, partially at least. Sugar, supplied in nature's own form as in fruits, grains and milk is much more easily and naturally used than concentrated sugar.

Berries have been found, in so far as they have been studied, similar in their dietary qualities to other fruits. Strawberries have shown a certain protective effect from scurvy in guinea pigs and are

CITRUS AND HEALTH

therefore rated as a good supply of vitamin C. Melons are classed with fruits in their dietary properties and have the same organic acids. They are not so rich in minerals and vitamins but they reveal many of the general fruit qualifications. Nuts have, in some way, possibly because of their attractive flavor, been compared with fruits as to dietary properties. They are, however, in this respect more similar to proteins and fats and among the richest of foods. Because of their concentration, they should be taken in small quantities as compared with fruits.

Not purely from a standpoint of nutritive value but because of their aid in the mechanical process of elimination and in the promotion of a hygienic intestinal condition, fruits are essential. Almost all other foods have been refined, or softened until only fruits and vegetables remain as our dependable supply of roughage so necessary in the digestive machinery. Other foods, for the most part, have been cooked, while fruit, because of its pleasing flavor and texture, survives as our fresh raw food, natural in its hygienic effects.

Therefore, in the promotion of greater consumption of fruit lies at least the partial solution of the problem of an adequate supply of minerals, organic acids, vitamins, and roughage essential to the well-being of animals, particularly of human beings.

Now in progress is an experiment that is showing striking results of what citrus fruit will do for teeth when taken in sufficient quantity. M. T. Hancke, Dental Research Association, Chicago, and of the O. S. A. Sprague Institute, University of Chicago, made careful records of 191 dental patients, only 17 of whom were free from trench mouth and pyorrhea, and found that of the 17, 16 had diets containing sufficient vitamin C. Of the 174 affected, not one was getting enough vitamin C (the scurvy-preventive). Of the 174 patients, 94 were lacking in vitamin C, only; all other vitamins were being supplied.

Accurate records were made of 104 of the patients and the following diet recommended: a pint to a quart of milk daily, plenty of meat, fresh vegetables and fruit, one or two eggs, a part of a head of lettuce and THE JUICE OF HALF A LEMON AND A PINT OF ORANGE JUICE DAILY.

Fifteen of the people failed to carry out directions and admitted the fact. Not one of the fifteen showed improvement. Eighty-five gave perfect cooperation and 85 made very evident improvement and many became cured in the period of less than eight months. Of 60 who had active progressive decay, all remained free from it for the period of the eight months' experiment. Unfilled cavities did not increase.

The diet prescribed other than citrus fruit juice is the usual diet required for normal nutrition. Other people have prescribed citrus fruit for the health of the teeth but this test is different in that it calls for greater quantity and the results reveal with what effects. The experiment is being continued for further truth.

FRUIT ZONES IN FLORIDA

Zone III—North Florida and Gulf Coast. This zone extends as far south as St. Augustine, Palatka, Gainesville.

Mulberry, pears, persimmons, plums, peaches, satsuma, orange, loquats, lime-quats, kumquats, calamondin, figs, quince, huckleberry, pomegranate, bunch grapes, muscadine, blackberries, dewberries, strawberries, blueberries, melons, haws.

Zone IV—Central Florida. This zone lies below Zone III and reaches, roughly speaking, from Vero southwest to Moore Haven, north to Davenport and Lake-land, and southwest to Bradenton. Some locations south of this are also included.

Avocado, mulberry, citrus, pears, peaches, persimmons, loquats, guavas, surinam cherry, fig, pomegranate, dewberries, blackberries, bunch grapes, muscadines, strawberries.

Zone V—South Florida.

Avocado, mulberry, mango, grapefruit, citrus, loquat, sapodillas, tamarind, rose apple, surinam cherry, guava, papaya, granadilla, carissa, pineapple.

NOTE—The above information as to fruit zones is according to Hume in "Gardening in the Lower South." Other fruits marked (S.) are grown only in the southern end of the state. A few others are marked (N.), indicating north Florida.

FLORIDA FRUITS AVAILABLE FOR HOME USE
AVOCADO

The avocado grows on a scraggly evergreen tree which blooms in March and April and fruits from July to January, depending on variety. Size, shape, color, and quality greatly vary. The size varies from 16 to 29 ounces. The skin is about one-sixteenth of an inch thick, very firm and tough. The firm, greenish-yellow flesh of buttery texture and nutty flavor makes one-half of the weight. One large seed in the center slips out easily, leaving just space for a salad filling or dressing of lime juice and a little salt.

There are three races—Mexican, Guatemalan, and West Indian. The Mexican, varying from 3 to 15 ounces, is hardiest and ripens from June to October. The color ranges from green to purple. The crushed leaves have an anise scent. The oil content is very high. The Mexican is thin-skinned and rather suited to local use. The Guatemalan is fairly hardy; the skin is thick, hard, and granular; the fruit, green to dark purple in color, is of splendid quality; the period of maturity is October to June. The West Indian avocado, grown only below Palm Beach and Fort Myers, is the commercial avocado of south Florida. It will stand but little frost. It is large, smooth and leathery skinned, of high quality, and ripens in late summer. The skin measures from one-sixteenth to one-sixty-fourth of an inch.

The avocado shows high percentage of solids, especially soluble solids due, in part, to oil which passes through linen filter. The caloric value is more than twice that of any other fresh fruit. Protein and ash rate high for fruit. There is a small amount of water and a high fat content. The acid is very low. The avocado is a good source of vitamins A and B. Protein and fat percentages in the avocado rank higher than that of any other known fruits.

Analysis of the West Indian avocado (seedlings) made by Jennie Tilt and May Winfield, Florida State College, Nutrition Research Laboratory, showed an average of 1.14 per cent for protein, 6.82 per cent for carbohydrate, 1.17 per cent for crude fiber, 1.02 per cent for ash.[1] The results obtained showed the West Indian avocado somewhat higher in moisture and lower in fat and protein than the Mexican and Guatemalan races.

The avocado is most palatable uncooked. It is often served on the half-shell, the flesh being scooped out with a spoon. It makes a nice, buttery spread for toast or crackers.

It is commonly served as a salad with salt and lime juice or salt and lemon juice. Some prefer orange or pineapple juice. Because of the buttery consistency of the fruit an oil dressing is too rich for avocado. Catsup, celery, nuts, onions are not good combinations for avocado. They destroy or conceal the delicate flavor. In its native land the avocado is much eaten by the Indians. They break it open, sprinkle

---

[1]The average moisture content found in mature fruit was 83.02 per cent and average fat content of West Indian (seedlings) was 8.09 per cent.

on a little salt and scoop out the pulp with corn cake called tortillas. Cooking or canning lessens the attractiveness as well as the flavor of the fruit. (Bulletin 24, Florida State Department of Agriculture.)

BANANA (S.)

The banana plant grows well only in South Florida. The Cavendish, brownish in color when fully ripe, is a dwarf variety bearing dense bunches of small fruit of very high quality. The Hart variety, taller, is also a good home use banana of fine flavor and texture.

This fruit, formerly considered "indigestible," has come into its own. The ripe banana is high in protein and also high in sugar content (about 20 per cent), being highest in the baking variety. The mineral content is not quite so high as the average avocado but is quite above the average for fruits. The indigestible factor in the banana, recent research shows, disappears with the complete ripening of the fruit, the stage at which it shows numerous brown spots. Whether it be due to the fact that the tannin becomes imprisoned in the ripened stage and therefore harmless, or to the fact that the raw starch nearly all turns to sugar in the ripening process, or to the effect on pectose, the fact remains true that cooking or ripening renders the banana easily digestible and suitable for adults, children and even babies. L. Von Meysenburg, M.D., Tulane University, says:

"In the feeding of the normal baby, banana is of value in supplementing the diet, aiding constipation and often stimulating the appetite. It may be given as early as the fourth month but must be thoroughly ripe and macerated.

"The banana is a good source of the pellagra-preventive factor. Through many experiments it has been found that, in scurvy or in symptoms leading to scurvy, the banana is curative. It is palatable and economical."

Banana supplements milk by supplying more vitamin C and carbohydrates needed by the child. It combines nicely in salads with citrus juices which give it an added acid flavor. About half an inch from each end should be removed as should also the "strings." Florida bananas have a finer texture and flavor than imported bananas. (Vol. 35, Bulletin No. 4, Florida State Department of Agriculture.)

BERRIES

Wild berries in north Florida include May-haw (red) and a Red-haw (red), ripening in the late summer; the huckleberry, blueberry, dewberries, blackberries, mulberries and youngberries.

Haws

The haws are small seedy berries growing wild on a shrub. They are best known for their use in making jelly of a wonderfully distinctive flavor and rich coloring. Some people have called the red-haw north Florida's cranberry.

Huckleberry

Huckleberries are different from Florida blueberries in that they contain the large seeds whereas the blueberry has many inconspicuous small seeds. The huckleberry shrub is smaller and scrubby. The huckleberry is good for pies, jellies and drinks.

Blueberry

The tall growing "Rabbit-eye" blueberry, of the huckleberry family, is the variety which has become famous commercially as the native blueberry of Florida plantings. The black, or blue-black fruit, borne in clusters, is $\frac{1}{4}$ to 11/16 of an inch in diameter. It ripens in late May or early June and lasts 10 or 12 weeks. The cluster does not all ripen at one time. This prolongs the "season" and requires weekly pickings. The acidity varies but is low. Sugar is about 7.5 per cent, mostly reducing sugar. It is not definitely determined but possible that the acid is citric. Blueberries combine nicely with orange juice in filling for pies. They are used alone in the fresh natural form or with sugar and cream.

Downy Myrtle (Berry)

This berry grows on a shrub. It resembles the huckleberry but has a thicker, richer juice. It makes a splendid jelly when 50 per cent acid guava is added.

Dewberry

The dewberry, growing on a low trailing vine and ripening earlier than the blackberry, is available for the family table early in the spring—the last of April or first of May. In the native growth they are more highly acid than the blackberry. For "deep pies" in early spring they have a popular place in north Florida menus. The jelly is welcomed as one of the first "spring jellies" in north Florida. In south Florida the Manatee dewberry has been cultivated with splendid results.

Blackberries

Blackberries grow wild throughout north Florida where the wild variety is much more popular in flavor for cooking purposes than the cultivated types. In southern Florida the blackberry has been cultivated. The Florida Marvel, found originally on the east coast, is a large, firm, good quality berry but lower in sugar than some other varieties. It is a splendid breakfast fruit served with sugar and cream. Juices, bottled in the natural form (or slightly sweetened) and processed at a simmering temperature, contain practically all the original food value of these various berries and to a large extent the natural flavor. In many sections all of these berries in the wild varieties "may be had for the picking" and the juices should be stored for the season when other fruits are "scarce." (See Fruit Juices.) (Vol. 37, No. 2, Florida State Department of Agriculture.)

Mulberries

Florida mulberries of some varieties bear through a period of several months. They are used by various methods as are other berries. There are the white, red and black varieties. The trees grow wild or cultivated. The fruit is very sweet, not having enough acid in the ripened stage for jelly. The seeds are too small to be noticeable.

Loganberries

A loganberry of rare quality is now being grown for local use and for market in west Florida, near Panama City. Its cultivation will no doubt become extensive in that section of the state.

Strawberry

The strawberry is Florida's most valuable berry. Needing a remarkably short period for growth and maturity, it can be grown very early in the warm climate and shipped advantageously.

This berry, being about 90 per cent water, appears to have a small per cent nutrients. Experiments have shown, however, that the strawberry, even when canned, is listed among those fruits having a very excellent vitamin content. An acid flavor and sufficient pectin in the slightly unripened fruit produces a good jelly but better known are the jam and preserves.

Elderberry (N.)

The elderberry grows on a shrub or bush 15 or 20 feet high. The berries grow in clusters. They have an acid flavor and make a refreshing drink and a good pie. They are often used as a cordial and as a coloring for other drinks.

North Florida Gooseberry

The north Florida gooseberry grows on a low plant. It is acid and suitable for pies.

Otaheite Gooseberry (S.)

This fruit grows on a tree in bunches like grapes not at the ends of the limbs but along the sides. The fruit is a yellowish color, acid, and makes a good jelly. South Florida has also a vine gooseberry.

SURINAM CHERRY

The Pitanga or Florida cherry, another name for the Surinam cherry, is a large, compact, bushy shrub with a green, glossy foliage which is wine color when new. The deep crimson ripe fruit, about one inch in diameter, is quite ornamental. It matures in southern Florida two or three times a year. It flowers first in February and fruits in from five to six weeks, the crop lasting about two weeks.

The soft, juicy, red flesh is of aromatic sub-acid flavor, pleasant in its natural form. Before ripening there is a resinous, pungent flavor. As the fruit ripens it turns from green to yellow, then orange and in the end a deep scarlet. The Florida type cherry is darker and has a more distinctive flavor not found elsewhere. Jellies, jams, and sauces made from this fruit have a unique flavor widely popular.

CITRUS

Citrus fruits contain the two essentials of every diet, namely: "What we should eat" and "What we like to eat." Minerals, vitamins, carbohydrates are there. The joy of the most pleasing flavor of all foods is there. Osborne and Mendel found that oranges, lemons and grapefruit contain as much vitamin B as milk and more than grapejuice, fresh apples and pears; that oranges and pineapples are good sources of vitamin A; that orange, lemon and tomato are highest of all foods in vitamin C. Experiments have shown in recent years that oranges play a big role in the building of teeth and in preventing decay.

Dr. Percy Howe, Forsythe Dental Clinic, Boston, Mass., through a series of experiments with monkeys, and Dr. M. T. Hancke of the Dental Research Association, Chicago, through recent tests with human patients, have found oranges most valuable in the building of teeth and in the maintenance of the health of teeth and gums. Chaney and Blunt, University of Chicago, have shown that increased orange juice in the diet has aided in the retention of calcium and phosphorus. They explain this efficiency on the part of the orange as being due to the fact that the orange maintains an acidity in the digestive tract and that it is alkaline in its residue, both conditions being conducive to the retention of calcium and phosphorus.

Orange juice as a mid-morning lunch for school children who were already getting a generous amount of milk in the home has been found to give Florida children a gain in weight and growth greater than that given by the same amount of milk to a similar group of children. The orange juice seems to help the child make better use of the milk he drinks and to give him a normal appetite. Orange juice concentrated, dried, fresh, or cold storage shows excellent supply of vitamin C. Orange juice is a good source of vitamin A and B.

Refreshing, appetizing, nourishing are the citrus fruits. They supplement milk. They give an alkaline balance. They are a mild laxative. Oranges are best fresh and undiluted; grapefruit is best in its natural state but it is also a success as a canned product. Lemons and limes are necessarily diluted as a drink. Kumquats and other small citrus products are used fresh or preserved. All citrus fruits may be used as preserves or crystallized products.

Kumquat

The kumquat, growing in bright, golden yellow clusters, is the smallest of citrus fruits, being only one to two inches in diameter. The thin rind is sweet and aromatic; the pulp is decidedly acid in certain varieties like the oval fruit of the Nagami or the round Marumi but the pulp of the round Meiwa is sweet. The fruit is eaten fresh; it is also preserved or candied whole. It is splendid for jelly or marmalade.

Citron

This citrus fruit grows on a tree similar to the lemon. Fruit is oblong, protuberant at the tip, 5 to 6 inches long, greenish-yellow in color and very fragrant. The pulp is acid and has a juice that may be expressed and used like lime. The rind, thick and spongy, may be candied and preserved. There is another fruit (a melon) by the same name used in somewhat a similar way.

Shaddock

The shaddock is the largest and coarsest of all citrus fruits. It has a thick rind and thick leathery septa between sections. It is suitable only for preserving and crystallization. It is sometimes pink inside. The juice is acid, bitter and scant.

Sour Orange

Sour orange has a thicker peel than the common orange. It is used for marmalades. The juice combines nicely in drinks with the sweet oranges.

CITRUS FOR DRINKS—Top: Kumquat with Foliage. Center: Grapefruit. Lower, left to right: Lemon, Lime, Sour Orange.

Bitter-Sweet

The bitter-sweet has a thicker peel than the sour orange and has a loose peel. It is used only for marmalades.

Limes

The lime is not a lemon but it is closely related to the lemon, orange, mandarin, pomelo and shaddock. Limes are more sensitive to cold and are therefore grown farther south. Most of the limes in Florida are on the keys south of the mainland. They are grown from seeds and therefore vary greatly in size, shape, flavor and juice percentage. They range in size from a medium-sized plum to a large-sized lemon. Lime juice is a good source of vitamin C. The Tahiti, a sprout of the Persian variety, a budded variety, has been grown on the mainland and found adaptable. It grows much larger. The rind is smooth, thin and green to yellow. The juice is almost colorless, good flavor, and strong acid.

West Indian lime grows on a thorny bush with rather small, light green foliage. Fruit is fine grain, juice plentiful, pulp soft, acid strong, flavor distinctly lime. The Palmetto Lime, a cross between West Indian and the lemon; and the Everglade Lime, a cross of West Indian with the Pomelo, are both good limes.

Rangpur Lime is hardier than the true lime. It is said to belong to Suntara orange group. Tree is small, thorny; foliage sparse. The fruit is medium size, rind rough, medium in thickness, easily separated from pulp and of irregular color; segments are easily separated; flesh is orange color; juice is plentiful, flavor agreeable.

The calamondin, a small round fruit growing on an ornamental hardy shrub, is sometimes erroneously called an orange but it is very closely associated with the lime. It combines nicely with the sweet orange in the preparation of a citrus drink. Lime juice is even more acid than lemon. It is 7 per cent citric acid. It also has an essential oil. Lime juice is used in medicine. It prevents scurvy and symptoms which precede the disease. It is used to supplement a diet necessarily short of fresh fruits and vegetables. Lime juice makes an excellent flavoring for many of the tropical fruits, for vegetables as well as for fish, meats, candies and desserts. It is also used to add flavor to various jams, fruits and jellies. Lime oil extracted from the rind is used in flavoring extracts and perfumery.

Limequat

The limequat is a cross between the lime and kumquat. It has a sweet rind and acid lime-like pulp. It is a hardy type, growing well in south central Florida.

Golden Lime

Golden Lime or Panama Orange is a small, round, thin-skinned, very juicy fruit. It is very sour but good flavor and makes a pleasing limeade. It is popular for marmalades, jellies and glacé fruits.

Lime Berry

Lime berry grows on a small bush. The fruit is edible and is like a small, dark red cherry. It makes a jelly of good acid flavor.

Lemons

Lemons in the original wild variety first found in Florida by early settlers are good only for root stock in high, dry land. The Ponderosa is too large to be of general commercial use, often reaching one to two pounds. The quality and flavor, however, are good. They are quite juicy and not a very thick skin. The regular commercial type of lemons is grown but the tendency is to grow too large. From the rind is produced lemon oil; the pulp, citrate of lime, citric acids and lemon flavoring. Lemon juice is one of the best sources of vitamin C. Even in cold storage, lemons show an excellent supply. Vitamins A and B are found in the peel and in fresh juice. Vitamin B is also found in the dried juice.

Pomelo—Grapefruit

The grapefruit is an excellent appetizer and probably contains "tonic" properties. Some have thought the grapefruit has an alkaloid all its own but chemists have not found it. Grapefruit juice both fresh and dried is a good source of vitamin B and an excellent source of vitamin C, equal to that of orange juice, lemon juice or tomato. The partitions in the fruit have a bitter taste. Improved fruits have eliminated the objectionable bitter and have left only the taste which lends individuality to the pomelo—that blending of sweet-bitter-sour that makes the fruit a pomelo. Those who know the flavor best call it the "pleasing personality" of the pomelo.

The early varieties of grapefruit are Duncan; mid-season, Florida Common and Walters; and late, Marsh Seedless. Foster and Thompson are the pink-fleshed varieties.

Oranges

Oranges are divided into two main classes, the common round orange of commerce known as "Mediterranean" and the Chinese or Mandarin or Kid Glove variety.

Mandarin

King Orange—King Orange (from Burma) is a large, rough, thick looseskinned fruit with a reddish, very juicy pulp of best flavor.

Tangerine—Tangerines (an excellent source of vitamin C) are of two main varieties, the flat red kind (Dancy) and a larger one, yellow in color (Oneco), a late variety.

Tangelo—Tangelos are hybrids—crosses between tangerine and pomelo. The tangelo has the qualities of both but is distinct from either. It is very juicy, of a rich, tart flavor. It has almost no fiber nor rag. The Thornton is one of the best varieties.

Satsuma—Satsumas are a hardy variety of the mandarin group, having been grafted on the trifoliata stock and are truly north Florida's orange.

Mediterranean

Among the varieties of Mediterranean oranges best adapted to Florida are the early oranges such as Parson Brown and Hamlin; mid-season varieties are seedlings, Pineapples, Enterprise Seedless and Jaffa; the late varieties are Valencia and Lou Gim Gong.

CHERIMOYA (S.)
(Jamaica Apple)

The cherimoya is of the annonaceous family of fruits, the annonas being tropical fruits composed of more or less coherent fleshy carpels or parts. The tree is of the small spreading type. The fruit, larger than an orange, is irregular in form and covered with small conical "bumps" or protuberances. The skin is thin and light green in color, changing to yellow; the flesh is white and of the melting texture. It has been called the "Masterpiece of Nature." Many brown bean-like seeds are imbedded in the flesh. The flavor is sub-acid, delicate and suggestive of the pineapple and banana. The fruit is purely a dessert fruit. The sugar content is very high being about 18¼ per cent. The protein and fiber are high and the acid content low.

BULLOCK'S HEART

This fruit, heart-shaped, is smooth and of a reddish brown when ripe. It is somewhat similar to the cherimoya and sugar apple but inferior in flavor.

SUGAR APPLE (S.)
(Sweet-Sop)

Sugar apple grows south of Palm Beach and Punta Gorda. The bush is similar to that of the sapodilla. The skin of the fruit is yellowish green, thick and rough. The fruit is pear shaped and the size of a man's fist. It is really a seed pod with numerous black seeds inside. The outside or surface is covered with "bumps." When the fruit is separated into carpels, of which it is composed, each rough section has a pure white or yellow meaty sweet and slightly aciduous pulp with the little black seed adhering. It is a custard-like dessert fruit. It is sometimes called the sweet-sop. It is similar to the cherimoya in composition, having a high sugar content, about 18½ per cent, but it is less piquant in flavor. It ripens in summer and is "in season" six months.

SOUR-SOP (S.)
(Guanabana)

This fruit is closely related to the sugar apple. The tree is rarely more than 20 feet high and grows only in the tropical section of the state. The fruit is the largest of the annonas (4 pounds). It is 6 to 8 inches long, rather an oval shape; a dark green color; a spiny surface. The flesh is white, juicy and aromatic. The texture is rather cottony. The flavor is a combination of mango and pineapple. It ripens in late spring.

The sour-sop is used for preserves, for preparations of sherbets and other refreshing drinks. The sour-sop sherbet is considered one of the finest in the world.

FIGS

The hardy Celeste is popular throughout Florida. It is a small, brownish-yellow, sweet fig (July 1). The Brown Turkey (July 15), white to pink inside, is a solid fig and hardy. The Brunswick (August and September) is a large violet-colored fig with thick, soft pulp.

Figs thrive best in sub-tropical localities but do well farther north if protected. They are grown largely in the vicinity of the "yard." The fruit contains a high per cent of sugar. Other nutrients are not abundant. The texture and flavor are pleasing. The fruit is best freshly picked from the trees. It needs no flavoring. The fig has a slight laxative effect. It is sometimes used with sugar and cream as a breakfast fruit. It lends itself to drying and preserving and canning. It is used in cookies, cakes and pastes, pudding, ice cream and other desserts.

GRAPES

Two types of grapes have done well on their roots in Florida—the muscadine and the summer grape. The former includes scuppernong, Thomas and James. The other type has developed into what is known as "bunch" grapes in Florida. The muscadines do not bunch and are, therefore, tedious to gather for shipping. The scuppernong grape has a flavor when fully ripe that is unexcelled. It is a russet color when ripe. The wild variety is a black grape of thicker skin and more meat

FLORIDA'S BUNCH GRAPES
(Courtesy E. E. Truskett, Monte Verde, Fla.)

but less juice. Both are splendid flavor in the fresh form and lend themselves to numerous ways of preparation. The Thomas is a reddish purple when ripe, while the James is purplish black. The "summer" grape (wild) grows in many of the Florida woods. It is quite acid and has enough pectin for jelly when not quite ripe. The flavor of wild grape jelly is a decided flavor, highly pleasing to both the Northern and Southern palate. The color adds to the palatability. Cultivated bunch grapes, such as Carmen, Ellen, Scott, Armalagar, are being successfully grown in Florida.

The many varieties, plus Florida's long season, make it possible to have on Florida menus good table grapes from June to September.

Grapes are high in sugar, varying from 15 to 35 per cent. The organic acids abundant in grapes act as a mild laxative and diuretic. Grape juice can now be sterilized at about 176° F, a temperature not high enough to injure the flavor or vitamin content. Fresh grapes, also grapejuice, have a fair amount of vitamins A and C as well as a very good showing in vitamin B. (Volume 37, No. 4, Florida State Department of Agriculture.)

GUAVA

Guavas, as grown in Florida, are of two groups—the Cattley guava, red and yellow, and the so-called Mexican guava. The red Cattley usually thrives wherever oranges grow well. The tree is an ornamental shrub of glossy leaves and reaches a height of 25 feet. The fruit, one to two inches in diameter, grows in large clusters. The purplish-red skin is thin; the sub-acid juicy flesh is white toward the center; the seeds are numerous. The Cattley guava has an aromatic flavor. It has not the mushiness of some other varieties. There is also a yellow Cattley guava of sulphur color and more delicate flavor, larger than the red Cattley. Mexican guavas are larger, being about the size of a hen egg and sometimes 3 or 4 inches long. Of the larger guavas there are the red, white and yellow varieties and of each of the three there are the sweet, sub-acid and acid types. All are very prolific.

There are as many varieties of guavas as of apples. The fruit ripens in late summer and fall and is "in season" several months. The analysis of the common guava has shown ash and protein to rate well in comparison with fruits in general. The sugar content is not high.

The guava, formerly known as a "jelly fruit," is now popular in the fresh, slightly cooked, and preserved forms.

GUAVAS

GRANADILLA OR PASSION FRUIT (S.)

(Small Pomegranate)

The granadilla is an ornamental vine fruit, oval in shape, 2 to 3 inches long and 1¼ to 2 inches thick, and deep purple in color when fully ripe. Inside the hard shell rind is a yellow, spicy, juicy, acid pulp within which are numerous small seeds, edible. The pulp is used in making drinks and for flavoring sherbets and ices. It needs sugar when taken in the natural form. The fresh fruit is served at the table and the juice is squeezed on the sherbet.

The yellow fruited passion fruit is similar to the purple but is larger and equally fine in flavor. Both fruits are used in cooking, as well as in salads.

LITCHI (S.)

The litchi grows on an ornamental tree. It has succeeded in the Miami section and, with a little protection, as far north as Bradenton. The fruit grows in clusters of 2 or 3 to 20 or more. They look a little like strawberries, being a deep rose when fully ripened and of the shape of the berry. The outer covering is scaly, hard and brittle. The seed is small. The flesh is white, translucent, firm and juicy and of sub-acid flavor similar to the muscat grape.

Analysis of the fruit has shown total sugar, 15.3 per cent; acid, 1.16 per cent; protein, 1.15 per cent; ash, .54 per cent; total solids, 20.92 per cent.

The fruit is picked in clusters with stems. They soon lose their pretty red color but they keep their flavor two or three weeks. Refrigeration takes care of them temporarily. The fresh fruit is very popular. It is both dried and preserved for future use.

MAMEY (S.)

The mamey is a dooryard tree of deep rich green foliage growing as far north as Palm Beach. The fruit is oblong or round and is 4 to 6 inches in diameter. It has a russet surface, leathery skin, a bright yellow, juicy, but firm, flesh of a sub-acid but pleasant flavor and a firm, close texture. It is sometimes stewed and sometimes sliced and served fresh with sugar and cream. Mamey preserve is popular and is similar to that made from apricot.

MAMMONCILLA OR SPANISH LIME OR HONEY BERRY (S.)

The mammoncilla grows on an erect tree 30 to 40 feet high and in clusters like grapes. This lime looks a little like a plum. The outer covering is thick, leathery and green. It has one large seed, the space between skin and seed being filled by a pleasant, edible, thick juice. It is not citrus. The pulp is a soft yellow. The flavor, in some varieties, is said to be sweet but it is often very acid.

MANGO (S.)

The mango tree is evergreen. Seedlings grow quite large but budded trees are smaller. Leaves are sometimes 10 to 12 inches long. The fruit grows on a long pendulous stem. It varies greatly in size from a small plum to 4 or 5 pounds in weight. It varies in shape from long, slender, to oval to round. The skin is smooth and from yellow to a deep yellow or apricot to a crimson. Some are only green. The aroma is spicy as is the flavor. The flesh, yellow to orange, is juicy and in the best sorts entirely free from fiber. It "melts in the mouth." The flavor is its own. It suggests an apricot and a pineapple but it is neither. It is mango—rich, luscious, acid, spicy. It is there, then it's gone—all gone—too soon. The seed is large, oval, flattened and contains a white kernel.

An analysis shows no starch apparent. The sugar content is high, varying from 11 to 20 per cent. Protein is higher than is usual in fruits. The acidity varies. The unripe fruit has very decided acidity. The ripe fruit is considered a laxative; the unripe, an astringent. The mango is a good source of vitamin C.

Both green and ripe products are used. The ripe fruit is eaten fresh as salad or dessert. Both kinds make splendid pies and are used in curries and sauces. The green or partly ripened pulp has considerable pectin and is good for preserves and jellies. It is sometimes boiled, strained, mixed with milk and sugar as a custard. The spicy sauces known as chutney are made of mangoes. The mango is used like the peach in canning. The budded type is the best texture for this purpose. The Haden and Mulgoba are popular types for eating fresh while the Sandersha is a type that lends itself to cooking. (Bulletin No. 20, Florida State Department of Agriculture.)

PAPAYA

The papaya, interestingly known as the tree-melon, in its best varieties, easily takes its place with the best of melons as to flavor and attractiveness. The tree has a straight, slender, spongy, leafless trunk which spreads into an umbrella-like tuft. The seedling quickly comes to the fruiting stage during the first year. Just below the "spread" the tree-melons cluster—sometimes as many as 20 or 30 of a size of 8 to 10 inches in length and sometimes weighing as much as 15 pounds. The fruit

BLUE STEMMED PAPAYAS
Bred and grown by Scott U. Stambaugh, Vero Beach, Fla.

is smooth, slightly ribbed and cylindrical in shape. As it ripens the skin turns from green to an orange yellow, while the sweet juicy pulp one to two inches in thickness becomes a deep yellow. Inside is a cavity filled with small, rough, dark peppercorn-like seeds which are enclosed in a thin mesh and slip out easily. So rapidly does the plant fruit that oftentimes green fruit, ripe fruit, buds and flowers are on the tree at the same time. The fruit begins to ripen in nine months. The crop is continuous through the bearing life of the tree when the weather is favorable. The papaya thrives in southern Florida where it has been grown for home and commercial purposes.

The papaya is a valuable source of vitamins A and C. Even in the green stage it shows almost no trace of starch and no tannin. The ash and protein are low as compared with the banana but they are quite constant. Sugar increases as the fruit ripens. The papaya contains a milky juice in which an active principal known as papain is present. It resembles animal pepsin in its digestive action.

As a breakfast fruit this tree-melon rivals even the honey-dew. The juicy pulp has a texture and a flavor its own, that starts the day "right" as well as "different." In south Florida where papayas grow and ripen in months of continual sunshine they make a valuable contribution to the diet of mankind. In a half ripened or green stage they may be cooked like squash, or, sweetened, they may be made into pies. The ripened pulp likes a dash of lime juice growing nearby but as "a first" for breakfast or as "a last" number for dinner it stands alone easily and successfully. In fact, whether they be down in the hammocks, along the canals or in a "set" grove they look just like the pictures and tickle the human palate for a taste. And later when after a night in the refrigerator they appear at breakfast in gorgeous orange yellow slices, or at lunch on a bed of green, garnished with a slice of lemon or lime, the "picture" becomes a most effective appetizer. Truly the lowly melon has been lifted up and glorified! The fruit has been successfully shipped to New York and California. (Bulletin No. 32, Florida State Department of Agriculture.)

PEACH

The Spanish or Honey type used in north Florida and the Chinese or "Peento" group of peaches has been grown successfully in south Florida. The peach, de-pending upon the variety, has a fairly high sugar content although it is about 85 to 90 per cent water. There is no appreciable amount of starch at any time but an increase in sugar upon ripening. Fresh peaches show a good content of vitamins A and C. By soil selection and adaptation of variety, Florida has learned to supply herself to some extent with peaches.

PEARS

The Pineapple and Hood pears are the most desirable Florida pears as to color, texture and uniformity. The Kieffer is adapted to north Florida. Pears are low in acid and need little sugar. Lemon or lime combine nicely with pear products. In the fresh form a fully ripened pear needs no additions. Raw fresh pears show some vita-mins B and C. For canning or for cooking, gather pears when fully grown but not entirely ripened. Keep in a dark, cool room for a few days for ripening. This process gives a finer grain texture and possibly a better flavor than the tree ripening process. When peeled, pears turn brown quickly, due to the action of an enzyme. A dilute saline solution (2 tablespoons salt to a gallon of water) prevents the coloring.

PERSIMMON
(Native)

The native persimmon, one to one and a half inches in diameter, grows almost all over the upper half of the state. It is highly stocked with tannin before the fully ripened stage but, when ripe, it is a very popular fruit, having a sugar content of about 15 per cent.

NOTE—The papaya (fresh leaves and stem) contains an enzyme (papain) which aids in the digestion of proteins. The natives of tropical islands use its juice to make meat tender in the cooking process. They wrap their fowls in its leaves or hang them overnight in the trees. Mothers, it is said, eat the papayas during lactation period to increase the milk supply for their babies.

JAPANESE PERSIMMON

This fruit is the cultivated persimmon used in Florida. It is much larger than the native fruit, ranging in size from two to four inches in diameter. The color varies from a light yellow to a deep reddish orange. The shape is, in some varieties, that of an apple flattened at the ends, and in others more of a pear shape with a pointed apex. The flesh is light yellow to dark according to variety.

The light flesh variety is good to eat only when fully ripe due to the fact that the pulp contains tannin. As the fruit fully ripens the tannin crystallizes and does not dissolve in the mouth. The dark flesh type has a pulp that is crisp, meaty like an apple and is edible before maturity. The sugar content in the ripe fruit is the highest of all common fruits—14 to 20 per cent—and is in the form of dextrose.

According to recent research by Jennie Tilt and Rebecca B. Hubbell, Nutrition Research Laboratory, Florida State College, seven varieties of Japanese persimmons show a range in average moisture content from 76.27 (Zengi) to 81.71 per cent (Tamopan); reducing sugar 11.55 per cent (Tsuru) to 17.39 (Zengi); protein .43 per cent (Tane Nashi) to .87 per cent (Okami); ash from .3 per cent (Tamopan) to .58 per cent (Tsuru); fiber from .11 per cent (Fuyugaki) to .49 per cent (Triumph). Tests were also made for vitamin B complex and the Tane Nashi, the fruit used, was found to be a very poor source of vitamin B complex.

The varieties most used are the Tane Nashi and the Fuyugaki. The former is round in shape with a pointed apex. It is from 3 to 3¼ inches long and nearly as broad. The skin is light yellow, shading to a bright, deep, yellowish-red as it ripens. The yellow flesh is astringent until the ripening period in August and September. The Fuyugaki, slightly flattened, deep red in color, is not astringent and can be peeled and eaten before it is fully ripe.

Persimmons are best used in the fresh form and are sweet enough for desserts. The pulp has been successfully used, however, in pies, sauces, and puddings as well as in ice creams. For pies, the non-astringent type is used when not fully ripe.

PINEAPPLE (S.)

Pineapple grows on a low, ragged plant with sword-like leaves. It perpetuates itself by lijos (scions) which grow out of the base of the plant near the ground and are called coronas. Pineapples from Fort Pierce south in Florida grow well in the open; in the other parts of south Florida they grow under slats. This is one of the most valuable of foods from a physiological standpoint. It contains a protelytic enzyme called bromelin which is closely related to trypsin. This ferment changes albuminous matter into peptones and proteoses and acts in acid, alkaline or neutral media. The flavor and odor of pineapples is due to the essential oils and ethers present in very small quantities. Pineapples should be allowed to stand on the plants until practically ripe. They lose little of their delicious flavor or of their food value in canning. They are rich, both in fresh and canned form, in vitamins A, B and C. (Vol. 37, No. 3, "Pineapple Culture," Florida State Department of Agriculture.)

PLUMS

Florida has a number of varieties of wild plums that still flourish, especially in north Florida. They are quite acid before ripening and make an excellent jelly, jam or butter at the half-ripened stage. Wild plum products have rare flavor and color that makes them most suitable to serve with meats or chicken.

Excelsior—Japanese plums crossed with some of Florida's native plums have given a few hybrids that are of splendid variety such as the "Excelsior," a wine-colored fruit with a firm yellow-red pulp of excellent quality and sub-acid flavor. The skin is thin and tough and neither bitter nor astringent.

McRae (Hybrid)—The fruit is a reddish yellow, has a juicy, yellow, sub-acid, firm flesh with an aromatic flavor.

Terrell (Hybrid)—This large plum, 2 inches in diameter, is wine-colored when fully ripe and has a greenish-yellow, meaty, slightly sub-acid flesh of excellent flavor and texture.

LOQUAT
(Japanese Plum)

The loquat grows on a small ornamental tree that branches two or three feet from the ground to form a dense crown. The white flowers are fragrant and ornamental. The fruit in loose clusters, are round or oval, one to three inches long, pale yellow to a beautiful orange in color, and downy on the surface. The skin is like that of a peach only a little tougher; the flesh is firm and meaty in some and "melting in the mouth" of other varieties and is a white to a deep orange color, juicy and of a "sprightly" sub-acid flavor. It is most commonly used as a fresh fruit but it may be stewed or jellied. Loquat pie made from partly ripened fruit favors of cherry pie. The seeds are removed before cooking. Unripe, the fruit is decidedly acid. The ripe fruit is sweet.

LANGSAT

This fruit is a plum something like the loquat. It is yellow, egg-shaped, about one to one and a half inches in length and better than the loquat.

CARISSA OR NATAL PLUM (S.)

The carissa grows on an ornamental thorny shrub. The scarlet fruit, one to two inches long and ovoid or egg shape, ripens mostly in summer but continues to appear through other seasons. As the fruit ripens it becomes a rich, dark red outside and inside. It exudes, when cut, a milky substance. This little plum is good for jellies and marmalades. Carissa sauce resembles cranberries.

POMEGRANATE

The pomegranate grows on a bush 15 to 20 feet high. The fruit is globular, the size of an orange or larger. It has a smooth, leathery skin which ranges from a yellow to a beautiful red in color. It is made up inside into several cells, each filled with many sided grains each of which is a transparent vesicle containing red juicy pulp and a seed. The flavor is sub-acid. Another variety (Purple-seeded) has an acid pulp. The fruit is very refreshing. It is used to prepare a cooling drink and to make jellies and marmalades.

QUINCE

The quince tree is a small, stiff, upright, little tree of hard-wood. The quince is one of the oldest known fruits. It has been less cultivated and is still hard and sour until cooked. The flavor of the cooked quince, however, is so agreeable that it is most popular as a jelly, marmarlade or flavor for other fruits. The quince is of a firm texture and is, therefore, used for preserving. The Chinese quince is a very much improved type.

RHUBARB

Rhubarb (according to Hume) is not particularly adapted to Florida's warm climate, but in recent years in south Florida it has been grown in early spring for home use and for local markets. "Immigrants" hail it with delight and pronounce it "good." Then it is good—tender, acid, appetizing—and makes just as good pies or sauce as if it were grown "north." The variety and season must of course be considered but the flavor is all there. Rhubarb has a medicinal value in that it is a laxative.

ROSELLE

The roselle plant resembles the okra and the cotton plant. It is often called the jelly okra. The edible portion is the bright red calyx, low in sugar (1%) and high in acid (3%). The only food value lies in the fine red color and the pleasant acid flavor—two rather valuable qualities. The calyces, if picked as soon as fully grown, make excellent ades, sauces, jelly or jam which are used in Florida to take the place that cranberries fill in many menus.

A plentiful supply of pectin and a generous acidity, combined with a cherry red color, give a wonderful jelly product equal to red currant or cranberry. For jelly, only ¾ of a pound of sugar (1½ cups) is needed for a pint of juice, secured by cooking and straining the fruit. Even after the seeds have ripened in the capsules the fruit may be used for jelly. The fruit may be dried without losing its jelly-making capacity. The young, tender shoots have been used successfully in jelly making and for "greens." (U. S. Department of Agriculture, Farmer's Bulletin 307.)

SAPODILLA (S.)

The sapodilla is a stately evergreen tree of 50 or more feet in height and grows well from Palm Beach south and up as far as the Manatee river on the west coast. The bark contains a milky latex called chicle, interesting commercially as the basis for chewing gum.

The fruit, round or oval in shape and from 2 to 3½ inches in diameter, looks like a potato, the thin skin being a rusty brown and slightly scurfy. The seeds, 10 or 12, slip out easily. Yellow brown, translucent, soft, sweet, and of delicious flavor is the ripened flesh. Unripened, however, the tannin and chicle are unpleasant. Someone has called the flavor of the ripe fruit "pear with brown sugar." Others have said, "it is maple syrup." It has about 14 per cent sugar. The odor is fragrant. There is a vitamin content of A and C.

MAMMEE SAPOTE (S.)
(Or Marmalade Plum)

This fruit grows on a tree (60 feet in height) of abundant light green foliage. The fruit is oval, 3 to 6 inches long. The skin is a russet brown, thick and woody. The flesh is firm and of a finely granular texture. The color is yellowish brown with a tinge of red, rather a rich saffron. There is in the center a large, hard, black and shiny seed which comes out as easily as the avocado seed. The flesh is rich and lacks acidity. It is similar to that of the sweet potato when cooked. Improperly ripened or inferior sapote has a squash-like flavor. In Havana it is used in sherbet and as a filler in guava cheese. In Central America the large seed is roasted and used to mix with cocoa in making chocolate. The sapote is best in its fresh, natural form. It has been used as a rich preserve. It has been called a "natural marmalade."

WHITE SAPOTE (S.)

The white sapote is now grown in Florida and while it belongs to the soft sweet fruits of the tropics it is liked by many Northerners. The fruit has a thin membranous skin, yellowish green and a yellow sweet melting flesh. It shows 20 per cent sugar. It is eaten fresh.

GREEN SAPOTE (S.)

The green sapote has a flavor similar to the sapota but more delicate, it is also of finer and smoother texture. The skin is thin, the flesh is darker but melting, sweet and juicy. The fruit is usually eaten fresh. There is also the sapote of the black variety.

STAR APPLE (S.)

The star apple is a dooryard tree and looks "like an evergreen peach." The leaves are a glossy green above a satiny brown underneath. Star apple fruit is round or oblate, something like an apple, and is from 2 to 4 inches in diameter. It is sometimes purple, sometimes a light green. When cut crosswise it shows a star-shaped interior. The flesh is in 8 segments in which the seed are imbedded. It is sweet and pleasantly flavored. Just under the skin is a layer of soft, somewhat granulous flesh and not very juicy. Inside this is a whitish flesh. Both are sweet—no acid at all. The fruit is usually eaten fresh. P. W. Reasoner described a dish called "matrimony." It is prepared by scooping out the inside pulp of the star apple and adding to it a glass of sour orange juice.

STRYCHNOS SPINOSA
(Natal Orange)

The tree looks like a scraggly, neglected orange. The fruit, on the outside, looks like a green orange and is about 3 inches in diameter. The outside is a hard shell. The pulp is rich, custard-like, about the consistency of a ripe banana, and has an aromatic flavor. The seed contains strychnine.

TAMARIND (S.)

The tamarind fruit (Indian Date) is a pod of a leguminous tree of ornamental small leaf foliage. The beans inside the pod are surrounded by a dark, pasty material, the edible portion of the fruit. This pulp has a sweetish-sour rather spicy flavor. Analysis shows 15 per cent acid (mostly tartaric) and over 40 per cent of reducing sugar. In fact it contains more acid than the sourest fruit and more sugar than the sweetest fruit. The taste, however, is distinctly sour.

Tamarinds are therefore used to make cooling sub-acid beverages, especially for invalids. The fruit is official in the pharmacopoeia as a laxative and refrigerant. Tamarind paste is a mixture of the pulp and about 75 per cent sugar. Mixing an ounce of tamarind pulp with 1½ pints of warm milk a nourishing beverage called tamarind whey is made. Young pods are sometimes cooked with rice and fish. The roasted seeds are said to be superior in flavor and valuable as a food product. Dried tamarind has a small amount of vitamin C.

In Key West the people pack tamarind in jars and cover with sugar sirup to keep on hand during the "off" season. They use the paste for making drinks when the fresh supply is exhausted.

The leaves contain an acid and furnish a dye stuff, also a quickly drying oil for paints.

CAROB BEAN (S.)

The Carob Bean or Locust Bean is sometimes used for stock feed. The ripe seeds are surrounded by a sweet mucilaginous mass used more as a confection than a food. The dried pod yields more than 50 per cent sugar.

Miscellaneous Sub-Tropical and Tropical Fruits

ABIU (S.)

The abiu resembles the canistel in growth and foliage but it has a light yellow fruit with white flesh. The skin is thick and tough. In flavor the pulp resembles the sapodilla but is a different texture.

AKEE (S.)

This fruit is a curious looking little capsule about three inches long and triangular in shape, and yellow and red in color. It contains three seeds with a whitish flesh at the base of each which resembles the brain of a small animal and which is firm, oily, and nutty in flavor. It is cooked with fish to give it an added flavor. Green or over-ripe akees should not be eaten at all. Fresh ripe akees are good food.

CACAO (S.)

The cacao ripens in June and in December and is limited to Monroe county. It resembles a short, thick cucumber 5 to 6 inches long and 3 inches thick. The pulp is pink to white, sweet, slightly acid. The rind is smooth, thick, tough and tasteless. The seeds or beans (20 to 40) are dried for market. They give an oil that acts as an anodyne.

COCOA PLUM (S.)

Cocoa plum is a small, edible, plum-like fruit, with a large seed, and has a cocoanut flavor.

CACTI

(1) Prickly Pear (S.), Indian Fig

The spiny fruit of 1 to 2 inches in length is pear shaped and red in color. It contains vitamin C. It is about 12 per cent sugar and about 85 per cent water.

(2) Cereus (S.)

(Summer Fruit)

Cereus fruit is oval, scarlet, 4½ inches in diameter. It also has vitamin C and 10 to 12 per cent sugar and 80 to 85 per cent water.

TI-ES OR CANISTEL OR VEGETABLE EGG

The canistel or ti-es (egg fruit) tree, a handsome bright green color, is a door-yard tree and grows well on the keys and as far north as Palm Beach. The fruit is round to oval and pointed at the apex. It is 2 to 4 inches long. The fruit ripens in summer. The membranous skin is yellow while the soft mealy flesh is a bright orange or egg shade. The flavor is rich and very sweet and the fruit is best fresh. When mature, it is best to take it from the tree and allow it to ripen in the house for three or four days.

CARAMBOLA (S.)

The carambola, growing on a small handsome tree about 30 feet high, is a bright yellow to golden brown oval shaped fruit 3 to 5 inches long, having 3, 4 or 5 longitudinal ribs and showing a star shape when cut crosswise. The pulp is astringent when green and acid when ripe. It has a fruity flavor and the odor of a quince. When slightly unripe it is used in jelly or pickles.

ILAMA (S.)

The ilama is said to be the best of the annonaceous fruits. It is smaller, reaching not more than one and one-half pounds. Pale green varieties have white flesh; the pink kinds have rose pink. Green varieties are sweet; the pink are acid. The fruit is used fresh like the sugar-apple. They ripen in summer. The season is short. The ilama belongs to the low lands and is more suited to south Florida than is the cherimoya.

POND APPLE (S.)

This fruit is sometimes called custard apple. It is no good as a fruit.

PITAYA (S.)

The pitaya is produced by a climbing cactus which bears night-blooming flowers. The fruit, about 2 or 3 inches in diameter, is crimson in color and strawberry in flavor. The flesh is white, juicy and seedy. It is used in making cooling drinks and sherbets or in the natural form.

ROSE APPLE (S.)

The rose apple grows on an ornamental plant. The fruit smells like a rose, is crisp and juicy. It is the color of apricot. It is round or oval and one or two inches long. The rose apple may be preserved or crystallized.

SATIN FRUIT (S.)

Satin fruit grows on a small tree whose leaves are glossy green on top and a burnished brown underneath. The purple fruit is about an inch and a half long and has a sub-acid flavor.

UMKOKOLO (S.)
(Kei Apple)

The umkokolo or kei apple grows on a vigorous, rich green, thorny shrub that flowers in spring and ripens in August to October. The fruit is nearly round, one inch in diameter and of a bright golden yellow color. The yellow, juicy pulp having an aromatic flavor of a high acid test when unripe, makes a splendid jelly.

WILD FIG (S.)

Wild fig trees, gigantic trees with green wax-like leaves, have small edible figs the size of a pea or larger.

BILIMBI (S.)

The bilimbi, similar to the carambola, is cylindrical, five angled, 2 to 4 inches long, greenish yellow in color, soft and juicy in texture. It is more acid than the carambola. It is used as a pickle or as a relish with meat or fish.

HORSERADISH TREE (S.)

The roots of this tree, when ground, have the odor and flavor of the herb horseradish. The leaves are used in curries.

JABOTICABA (S.)

This fruit resembles grapes and grows on the body of the tree which grows to a height of 60 feet. The juice makes an excellent drink or jelly.

JUJUBE (S.)

The jujube is a small spiny tree about 20 feet high and very prolific. The fruit is about the size of a date. It has a brown thin skin and a sweet white flesh of mealy texture inclosing a hard two-celled seed. It ranks high (about 21½ per cent) in sugar. The fresh fruit (best varieties) is good to eat in natural form. Dried it resembles the date in form and flavor. It may be boiled with rice, stewed or baked, made into bread as raisins, boiled in honey and sugar as a glacé product. It is used commercially as a flavoring for confections. Chinese varieties, Yu, Mu Shing Hong, and the Lang, are best, according to Popenoe.

KETEMBILLA (S.)

(Ceylon Gooseberry, *Aberia Gardnerii*)

This fruit grows on a shrub similar to, though more slender and less vigorous than the umkokolo. It is maroon in color and has a velvety surface. The pulp, sweet and luscious, resembles in flavor the English gooseberry. It is a better fruit than the umkokolo and makes a fine jelly or preserve. The season is winter.

MONISTERA DELICIOSA (S.)

Monistera Deliciosa is the fruit of a monster vine-like plant that has a bloom similar to a lily and an openwork leaf. The vine has many air roots. It also sends down tubes deep into the ground to get water. The fruit itself resembles in shape a very large ear of corn. The big plump kernels, juicy and sweet, are in a case that is edible. The arrangement is like that of "corn on the cob." The color is green. The fruit stands straight on the vine until ripe. It then turns down. The flavor is a combination ripe banana and fresh strawberry with just a little of the snap of pineapple. It may be eaten plain or with sugar and cream.

PARA GUAVA (S.)

The Para guava, not strictly a guava but horticulturally classed with the guava because of its similarity, is a sulphur yellow fruit, oval or round, and 2 to 3 inches long. The soft whitish pulp, acid but pleasant in flavor, has a few seeds larger in size than the true guava. It has little of the musky aroma of the guava.

CASHEW (S.)

The cashew grows south of Palm Beach and Punta Gorda. This is a fruit and a nut combined. It is a small, oddly-shaped yellow fruit 2 or 3 inches long of pyramidal form and bears at its distal end the nut or seed. The flesh part of the fruit is called the cashew apple. This arrangement of the seed outside the pulp is most unusual. The nut or seed, about one and one-half inches in length, is kidney shaped and is enclosed in a grayish brown cellular coat that contains an essential oil which, when cooked, has a burning effect on the skin. It is roasted before it is eaten. The skin of the appie, very thin and easily broken, is a bright yellow or flame scarlet. The flesh is soft, juicy, acid and a light yellow color and has a pungent aroma. It is used as a preserve or jam of highly pleasing quality and also as a drink. The nut, when roasted, has a chestnut flavor. The meat is of fine texture and good quality. A nutritious oil similar to almond oil may be expressed.

IMBU (S.)

The imbu looks somewhat like a green Gage plum. Oval shaped, it is one and one-half inches long and greenish yellow in color. It grows wild and is very productive. The fruit makes a splendid jelly. The skin is thicker than that of a plum and tough. The flavor of the soft juicy flesh is akin to a sweet orange when ripe but is acid when not fully ripe.

AMBARELLA
(Otaheite Apple)

The ambarella is a straight, tall, stiff tree which in some countries grows as high as 60 feet and with leaves 12 inches long but not so large in Florida. The fruit, some two inches long, oval in shape, is a pretty orange yellow. The skin is something like that of the mango but tougher. The flesh is firm, juicy and pale yellow, of a sub-acid flavor and sometimes resinous. The queer looking seed is covered with bristles which hold the flesh tightly. The clusters (of 2 to 10) hang on long stems. They ripen in winter and are not quite so good a flavor as the imbu. The sugar content is about 10½ per cent. There is very little fiber. Much depends upon variety. The best do not compare with the mango but rank very well as a wild fruit.

IV—Uses of Florida Fruits and Vegetables

1. COCKTAILS, SHERBETS AND DRINKS

PAPAYA COCKTAIL

Cut papaya in dice and serve in glasses with orange, lemon or lime juice, and a little sugar and chipped ice.

PAPAYA SHERBET

Mix four cups papaya pulp with two cups sugar and juice of three lemons and freeze. Add a little sugar if desired.

MELON-PEACH COCKTAIL

Fill half a small cantaloupe (chilled) with sliced peaches. In the center fill with seeded grapes, blueberries or blackberries. Sprinkle freely with lemon and orange juice combined or with slightly sweetened lemon juice.

GRAPEFRUIT-PEACH SHERBET

To crushed peaches add one can grapefruit hearts (cut in small pieces). Sweeten to taste and freeze.

ORANGE JUICE COCKTAIL

4 small oranges	½ cup strawberries
Few grains salt	½ cup crushed pineapple
1 teaspoonful lemon juice	Sugar to taste

Cut a thin slice from the tops of oranges. Remove pulp and juice. Add strawberries, lemon juice and sugar to pulp and juice of oranges. Fill peel and set on ice and leave until thoroughly cold. Serve in glasses surrounded with crushed ice.

FRUIT COCKTAIL

Place 4 tablespoonfuls of fresh peaches in cocktail glasses. Add 4 tablespoonfuls of grape, pineapple or any berry juice. Sprinkle with nut meats. Fill dish with shaved ice. Serve.

FRUIT PUNCH

1 cup sugar	1 pint grape juice
½ cup water	2 cups crushed pineapple
½ cup lemon juice	Lemon or orange slices
½ cup orange juice	

Cook sugar and water 5 minutes. Cool. Add fruit juices and pineapple. Serve with plenty of ice and garnish with slices of lemon or orange.

ORANGE FRUIT CUP

½ cup orange juice	¾ cup diced pineapple
2 tablespoons lemon juice	¾ cup of one of the following fruits:
2 tablespoons pineapple syrup	White grapes, strawberries,
Sugar	peaches, pears, cantaloupes,
¾ cup orange pieces	bananas.

Combine fruit juices and sweeten to taste, keeping rather tart. Add mixed fruits. Place on ice. Serve very cold in cocktail or sherbet glasses. Garnish each serving with Surinam cherry, strawberry, carissa cut in half, or loquat slices. Use mint if fruits are not in season.

Oranges should have all membrane removed. If grapes are used, seeds should be removed. If strawberries are used, cut in half. Peaches or pears, if used, should be diced; cherries should be stoned; cantaloupe or bananas should be cut in balls or small sections.

GRAPE AMBROSIA

Soak 4 tablespoonfuls of gelatine in 1 cupful of grape juice for 10 minutes, then heat over hot water until dissolved; cool and add ½ cupful of shredded orange and ½ cupful of shredded pineapple. Beat 1 pint of cream until stiff and add ½ cupful of sugar. Beat the whites of 2 eggs until stiff and dry and add ⅓ cupful of sugar. Combine the two mixtures and beat into gelatine, pour into cold individual molds and place on ice until ready to serve. Turn out on a slice of pineapple and garnish with whipped cream.

SHRIMP AND PINEAPPLE COCKTAIL

1 cup cooked shrimp (fresh or canned)   Mayonnaise dressing
2 cups canned pineapple tidbits   Lemon juice

If shrimp are large, cut them in halves. Sprinkle with lemon juice and chill thoroughly. Drain and chill pineapple. Combine shrimps and pineapple and mix with well-seasoned mayonnaise dressing. Serve in sherbet or cocktail glasses.

LIME COCKTAIL SAUCE FOR SHELL-FISH

1 tablespoon prepared horseradish   6 tablespoons lime juice
3 tablespoons tomato catsup   ¼ teaspoon tabasco sauce
1 teaspoon salt   Oysters or clams

Mix sauce ingredients thoroughly and pour over oysters or clams arranged in cocktail glasses.

Sauce may be served in baskets made from lemon rinds, the fish being served on the half shell. Serve very cold.

CITRUS COCKTAIL
(Serves 8-10)

¼ cup lemon juice   Few grains salt
¼ cup grapefruit juice   Cracked ice
¼ cup orange juice   Mint sprigs
¼ cup sugar dissolved in water

Combine fruit juices, sugar, salt and water. Pour over cracked ice in cocktail glasses and serve garnished with mint sprigs.

ICED ORANGE APPETIZER
(Serves 8)

2 tablespoons gelatine   ¾ cup sugar
4 tablespoons cold water   2 tablespoons lemon juice or lime
3 cups orange juice   1 cup orange pulp

Combine gelatine and cold water. Heat 1 cup of the orange juice over hot water. Add gelatine and sugar. Stir until dissolved. Cool. Add rest of fruit juices. Chill several hours. Stir occasionally. Add orange pieces. Serve ice cold as first course. Garnish with mint sprigs.

GRAPE JUICE LIMEADE

Juice of 5 limes   3 cups of water
1 cup sugar   2 cups grape juice

Place ice in pitcher. Add sugar and water; stir thoroughly. Add grape juice and last the lime. Let stand several minutes before serving.

LIME JUICE COCKTAIL

4 tablespoonfuls of lime juice   2/3 cupful of ginger ale
2 tablespoonfuls of orange juice   Crushed ice
2 tablespoonfuls of sugar syrup

Place ingredients in cocktail shaker; shake, and pour over crushed ice in four cocktail glasses. Serve.

AFTERNOON TEA

3 teaspoonfuls of tea

2 cupfuls of boiling water

1 lime

Cloves

Loaf sugar

Sprigs of mint

Make the tea in teapot or with tea ball; let stand for several minutes; then serve, placing in each cup a slice of lime pierced with a clove. Add a cherry and serve sugar separately in such quantities as may be desired.

FRESH LIMES

To keep limes for several weeks: Select clean, sound fruit, picked with stem buttons on. Place in air tight fruit jars. Lime juice extracted, strained after it settles, may be filled into jars, corked and kept for several months.

LIME SYRUP

(For cold drinks, ice cream, sauce, etc.)

2 dozen ripe limes

1 pound of cube sugar

½ cupful of water

Wash the limes thoroughly in cold water and dry. Rub the sugar vigorously all over the lime until it loses its color. Squeeze the juice on the sugar, add water; then bring almost to a boil and strain. For cold drinks, place 2 tablespoonfuls of the syrup in a tumbler with crushed ice and fill with plain water.

LIME WITH FISH

Squeeze juice of two limes over fish when ready to bake. Add more lime juice while fish are baking, if desired. Garnish with parsley and slice of lime. Serve fish with sauce.

TOMATO JUICE

Ripe tomatoes (red) should be slightly heated and pressed to obtain pulp with juice. A dilver or sieve may be used for home use with cold tomatoes. The juice loses its attractiveness without the pulp.

FRUIT PUNCH FOR A CROWD

2 quarts sugar

1 quart water

2 quarts tea, weak

1 quart lemon juice

1 quart orange juice

1 quart grape juice

1 quart of pineapple (grated)

Ice water

1 cup strawberry slices

2 cups fancy orange slices

Make syrup of sugar and 1 quart water. Make tea infusion by pouring 2 quarts (8 cups) boiling water over 5 tablespoons tea. Cool. Combine syrup, tea, fruit juices and water. Add strawberry slices and orange slices, which may be cut in fancy shapes or simply halved or quartered.

Punch may be strained before adding strawberry and orange slices, but this will lessen quantity made. Less water may be used and punch poured over block of ice in punch bowl. When strawberries are out of season, the strawberry slices may be replaced by another cup of orange slices. Recipe may be halved or quartered to serve a smaller group.

UNDERWEIGHT ADE

1 egg yolk

¾ cup orange juice

¼ cup thin cream

Sugar if desired

Beat egg yolk until light, add orange juice and blend thoroughly. Pour into glass and stir in cream. Sweeten to taste. Serve at once.

FRUIT JUICE PUNCH

Sweeten milk with sugar and add two tablespoonfuls or more of any of the fruit juices—lime, grape, loganberry, pineapple, grapefruit. Beat well before serving, and add a beaten egg white and a dash of nutmeg or cinnamon, or a dab of whipped cream for each glass.

LEMON MILK
(Serves 2)

Juice of 1 to 2 lemons
1 pint milk

Beat juice of lemons and milk together with a whirl type beater or put in a glass jar and shake well. Serve immediately.

This is a substitute for buttermilk and makes a healthful drink tolerated by weak digestions. It must be mixed each time served, as curd and whey of milk will separate if allowed to stand. More or less lemon juice may be added, depending upon sourness desired for drink.

LEMON EGG-NOG
(Serves 1)

6 tablespoons milk	2 tablespoons sugar
½ cup cold water	2 tablespoons lemon juice
1 egg	Grated nutmeg

Combine milk, water, egg and sugar. Beat thoroughly, pour in lemon juice and mix vigorously. Serve in a large glass topped with a grating of nutmeg.

ORANGE CREAM PUNCH

To two cupfuls of whole milk and two cupfuls of thin cream add two teaspoonfuls of lemon juice, one cupful of orange juice and sugar to taste. Fold in the beaten whites of four eggs and serve at once. This is best if served very cold, provided the children are willing to sip it slowly. Any fruit juice may be substituted for the orange juice, but the lemon juice is usually required to bring out the flavor.

2.   FRUIT AND VEGETABLE HORS D'OEUVRES

Orange sections rolled in toasted cocoanut.
Orange sections spread apart like a flower and center with fruit, mayonnaise and nuts.
Berries and small pear halves. Roll in chopped mint.
Pineapple sections. Roll in crushed nuts.
Banana sections. Marinate in lemon or lime or sour orange juice. Roll in peanuts.
Lemon baskets: Fill with salted pecans and candied kumquats.
Papaya marinated with lime juice. Serve in slices.
Curled celery. Radish roses. Small yellow or red tomatoes stuffed with celery and snappy cheese.

3.   SALADS

A.   Preparation of Fruits and Vegetables for Salads

Greens

1. Select tender greens in the early morning. Cut off roots, remove coarse leaves.

2. Keep them in a cool place in a closed vessel or closely wrapped in paper or a paper bag. Sprinkle the lettuce head lightly and place in a paper bag.

3. Wash leaves thoroughly in two or three waters. Watercress and lettuce need careful attention. Green insects often infest them. Lift the leaves out of one water into the other.

4. Crisp the greens in very cold water for ½ hour or less. Acid (vinegar or lemon) added to the water for crisping destroys insects. Salt wilts greens.

5. Drain, spread on a towel or place in a covered dish and set in a cool place until serving time. Shake dry.

6. Cut out the stem end or core of head lettuce, about one inch, and let cold water run into the opening. Turn the head right side up to drain. The leaves will separate readily and be crisp and dry for serving.

7. To make a nest of lettuce, use leaves of different sizes, beginning with larger leaves and fitting into them one or two smaller leaves, keeping the leaves cupped and the stem ends together.

8. To shred leaves roll them into a firm roll. Shred with a silver or stainless steel knife or with scissors. Shredding should be done just before combining.

9. Shred cabbage fine with a long, thin knife. Crisp in cold water; drain.

10. To keep parsley, sprinkle it with cold water, put it in a tight fruit jar, and keep it in a cool place.

11. Combine a "green" salad with dressing just before serving.

Oranges or Grapefruit

1. To section oranges or grapefruit, cut a thick layer off the top and one off the bottom of the fruit and then cut off sections of peel from the sides, cutting deep enough to remove all white membrane and to leave the fruit exposed. With a sharp knife cut out each section separately.

2. To peel grapefruit, let it stand in hot water 5 to 10 minutes, and then cool.

Tomatoes

1. To peel tomatoes:
    a. Draw over the surface of each tomato the edge of a knife. Peel.

WATER CRESS

b. Place tomatoes in a colander. Dip them in boiling water. Cool. Peel.

2. In cutting tomatoes, section them into quarters, sixths or eights, cutting not quite through, or slice in generous thick slices.

Celery

1. Wash with a stiff brush.

2. To curl celery, cut stalks in 3- or 4-inch lengths. Feather the ends and place in acid water (2 tablespoonfuls vinegar or lemon to 1 cup water) for 20 minutes.

Carrots

Grind young carrots with finest cutter of the grinder or grate.

Radishes

Leaving one inch of stem, peel half way down to stem and leave radishes in very cold water to crisp. Drain.

Onions

Peel under water and from the root upward.

Nuts

To break or crush, place nuts in a paper bag and roll with rolling pin. Add nuts last before serving the salad.

Cream

To whip cream, use Dover egg beater in deep bowl. Make wrapping paper cover by slashing and slipping over egg beater handle to fit bowl. Be sure cream and bowl are well chilled.

To whip evaporated cream, place can in cold water. Bring to a boil and boil for a few minutes. Cool quickly or place in the refrigerator to get very cold. Whip in small quantities.

B. Salad Dressings

General Directions

1. All salads are grouped under four main needs. Others are variations:
a. Mayonnaise.
(Cream may be added.)
b. French.
c. Cream.
d. Cooked.
(Cream may be added.)

2. Remove spoon or fork from salad dressing. Use an enamel or bright aluminum pan for cooking.

3. Use all of eggs instead of two yolks if desired.

4. Lemon juice may be replaced by the juice of the calamondin, sour orange or lime, and any one of these juices with a little salt (and possibly a little sugar) may be used alone as a dressing for Florida salads.

MAYONNAISE
(Makes 2¼ cups)

1 egg yolk	½ teaspoon salt
2 tablespoons sour orange or lemon juice	2 cups salad oil

Stir egg yolk, salt and 1 tablespoon lemon juice until well mixed. Beat in oil, slowly at first until ¼ cup is added, using a whirl type beater. Then add oil more rapidly. When dressing becomes thick, add remaining lemon juice and proceed with remainder of oil.

For sharper, thinner dressing, add 2 extra tablespoons lemon juice just before serving.

CREAM MAYONNAISE
(Makes about 1⅓ cups)

To 1 cup mayonnaise add ⅓ cup whipped cream and ¾ tablespoon lemon juice. This is an excellent fruit salad dressing.

TARTAR SAUCE

To 1 cup of mayonnaise add 3 tablespoons finely chopped pickles and 1 table-spoon chopped parsley.

HONEY DRESSING

Add (instead of sugar) a small amount of tupelo, palmetto or orange blossom honey.

THOUSAND ISLAND DRESSING

To one cup of mayonnaise add:

2 tablespoons chopped pepper or pimento	½ cup of Chili sauce
2 tablespoons chopped or scraped onion	½ cup chopped celery

Add whipped cream or beaten egg whites (if desired).

Other Variations

Chopped red or green pimento, avocado pulp, tomato catsup or paste, a little red jelly, a hard cooked egg yolk, or beet juice may be added to give color.

FRENCH DRESSING

Use a tightly closed jar for mixing large amounts. Keep in refrigerator until ready to use.

RECIPES
(Makes about ½ cup)

3 tablespoons lemon juice	¼ teaspoon paprika
6 tablespoons salad oil	¼ teaspoon salt

Stir or shake thoroughly before serving.

FRENCH HONEY DRESSING

To French dressing add 2 tablespoons strained honey. Serve on fruit salads.

FRENCH FRUIT DRESSING
(Makes about ½ cup)

3 tablespoons lemon juice
3 tablespoons orange juice
4 tablespoons oil
Mix all ingredients thoroughly.

¼ teaspoon salt
½ teaspoon sugar or honey

CHEESE DRESSING

To French dressing add gradually 2 tablespoons of some cheese of piquant flavor as Roquefort or snappy cheese which has been rubbed to a cream. Blend until smooth.

OTHER VARIATIONS FOR PLAIN FRENCH DRESSING

1. Add ½ tablespoon chopped parsley and 1 teaspoon pimento.
2. Use calamondin juice instead of lemon.
3. Add 1 teaspoon mustard, ½ teaspoon onion juice, 1 tablespoon Worcestershire sauce.
4. Add chopped onion, bell pepper, celery, (Parisian).
5. Add 2 tablespoons Surinam, roselle or carissa jelly.
6. Add 2 tablespoons horesradish (grated).
7. Add 2 tablespoons peanut butter before shaking.
8. Add one grated egg yolk.

CREAM DRESSING

1 cup thick cream, sweet or sour
4 tablespoons lemon juice
1 to 2 tablespoons sugar

1 teaspoon salt
¼ teaspoon paprika

1. Beat the cream with an egg beater until smooth, thick and light.
2. Mix the other ingredients together and gradually add the cream, beating all the while.

FRENCH SALAD DRESSING NO. 1

Two whole eggs, juice of 1½ lemons, ½ cup honey or thick syrup from spiced peaches or pears; or ½ cup fruit juice sweetened or thin syrup from canned fruit, few grains paprika, few grains salt.
1. Beat the egg slightly, combine with honey and lemon juice, and add paprika and salt. Cook in a double boiler until thick.
2. Cool and fold in 1 cup whipped cream (sweet or sour) or less thin cream.

FRENCH SALAD DRESSING NO. 2

2 tablespoons sugar
2 tablespoons lemon juice
Paprika.

1 egg or two yolks
Whipped cream

Beat the eggs. Add the sugar and lemon juice.
Cook in a double boiler until the mixture thickens.
Cool. Add the whipped cream.

COOKED DRESSING
(Makes 1¾ cups)

2 eggs
4 tablespoons flour
2 tablespoons sugar
1 teaspoon salt

¼ teaspoon paprika
1¼ cups cold water or milk
⅓ cup lemon juice
1 tablespoon butter

Beat the eggs slightly. Stir in all dry ingredients. Add water. Cook in saucepan 'till thickened, stirring constantly. Add butter and lemon juice. Cool.
This is a salad dressing without oil and is liked especially by children.

C. Salad Combinations
1. Vegetable Salads

Various combinations may be made of cooked and raw vegetables but the real vegetable salad serves to add fresh uncooked food in its natural state.

1. Combination:
   Radishes, pepper, onion, tomato, cucumber on lettuce or greens. French dressing.
2. Tomatoes with celery and pepper.
3. Coleslaw:
   Chopped cabbage with green peppers and peanuts, cream dressing or a mayonnaise with cream added.
   Sliced, firm, crisp pear or apple adds to the flavor.
4. Cabbage, pineapple and pecans.
5. Cabbage, carrot, celery and peanuts. Omit celery and use fig preserves if desired. French dressing; or to the dressing add peanut butter.
6: Tomato—top with sour cream dressing sprinkled with parsley. Garnish with strips of green pepper.
7. Any salad green, young and tender, combines with a dressing made of hot bacon fat, lemon juice and grated hard cooked egg.

2. Fruit Salads

1. Grapefruit, celery, red or green sweet pepper, French dressing.
2. Grapefruit, celery, pecans or crushed peanuts, French dressing.
3. Grapefruit sections arranged overlapping in a circle on lettuce. Use French dressing or Parisian dressing.
4. Grapefruit or pineapple, 1 cup orange cubes, $\frac{1}{3}$ cup crystallized citrus fruit, 3 tablespoons pecans, fruit salad dressing.
5. Grapefruit (one), oranges (two), lettuce, avocado (cubes), alternate sections of oranges or grapefruit, in circle on lettuce. Place avocado cubes in center. French dressing.
6. Orange sections arranged in circle on lettuce. Strawberries heaped in center. Fruit or cream dressing.
7. Orange cubes heaped into and around a guava cup. Top with strawberries or Surinam cherries. Fruit dressing.
8. Sliced orange with crystallized or fresh fig, pecan nuts.
9. Orange sections circled around a mold of carissa or Surinam cherry jelly garnished with a sprig of mint.
10. Orange and pineapple cubes with strawberries. French dressing.
11. Orange sections rolled in cocoanut arranged on green leaves. Garnish with Surinam cherries or with preserved or crystallized carissa.
12. Orange sections cut in pieces. Florida Amalga grapes (seeded), crushed peanuts or pecans.
13. Grapefruit, orange, tangerine sections with occasional cubes of pineapple or Florida banana with a sprinkle of lemon juice.
14. Satsuma section with preserved figs, pecans, pomegranate juice. Avocado and tomato or tomato jelly with nuts.
15. Avocado, celery and grapefruit.
16. Guava cups stuffed with strawberries or with congealed guava pulp and pecans. Use cream dressing (sweetened). (Marinate cup with lemon to prevent darkening.)
17. Guava, celery, cheese, with fruit dressing.
18. Guava, pineapple, pecans, crystallized fig.
19. Mango (non-fibrous type, such as Haden) with juice of lemon, lime, passion fruit, or sour-sop.
20. Tangerine lobes, ground pecans served with fruit dressing.
21. Banana marinated in lemon or sour orange juice, crushed peanuts, ripe strawberries, fruit dressing.
22. Halves of peach, pear or guava, center filled with cheese, topped with carissa or Surinam cherry.
23. Carissa (halves), slices of crystallized kumquat rolled in cocoanut.
24. Pineapple, celery, nuts.
25. Sliced pineapple filled and heaped with strawberries. Cream dressing.
26. Pineapple, seeded grapes, loquats or carissas (halved) with or without pecans.

Florida Fruit Special

Setting:
    Escarole, Florida's Loose Lettuce.

Fruit:
    Pink Grapefruit with Strawberries.

Dressing:
    French with Fruit Juice or French cream dressing.

PLATE I

Tropical Salad

(Main luncheon dish)

Setting:

    Florida Lettuce with sprigs of Parsley.

Center:

    Avocado with Tomato Pulp dressing, topped with Pecan.

PLATE II

Luncheon Salad

Setting:

    Lettuce Leaves with Cucumber and Pepper Rings, Radish Roses, Lemon Slices and Tomato Quarters.

Center:

    Mound of Shredded Cabbage and Grated Carrot, marinated.

Dressing:

    French or Mayonnaise.

NOTE: This salad with a drink and bread and butter constitutes "a whole meal."

PLATE III

Dinner Salad

Fresh Florida Relish

Leaves of Head Lettuce with Water Cress and Celery, Slices of Onions, Green
Pepper Rings, and thinly sliced fresh Winter Cucumbers.

Tart French Dressing.

PLATE IV

Pineapple-Tangerine Cup

Setting:

    Lettuce with Water Cress and Mint leaves garnished with Hillsboro Straw-
        berries.

Cup:

    Pineapple with top removed.

Filling:

    Pineapple tidbits, celery, and tangerine cubes finished with a circle of tan-
    gerine lobes centered with a strawberry on a mint leaf.

Dressing:

    French with Fruit Juice or Fruit Cream dressing.

PLATE V

Florida Dessert Salad

Setting:

    Lettuce leaves with Water Cress.

Center:

    Whole Preserved Figs, drained and stuffed with Cream or Cottage Cheese.

Garnish:

    Pecans.

NOTE: Fresh Florida Sugar Figs should be used when in season.

PLATE VI

SPECIAL GARNISHES FOR FLORIDA SALADS

1. Green or red peppers, strips or small pieces.
2. Surinam cherry, carissa plum, any number of crystallized citrus fruits (kumquats being especially appropriate).
3. Natural color jellies of carissa, roselle, Surinam cherry, tamarind, May haw, fall haw, guava, wild grape and many other Florida fruits.

SETTINGS FOR FLORIDA SALADS

Curled celery, endive, Romaine, curly lettuce, spinach, beet greens, "tender greens," kale, young mustard, water cress, mint, parsley, lemon, kumquat, fresh tender cucumber strips or rings, mild-flavored onions, nasturtiums, pineapple shells,

ROMAINE—WHITE PARIS COS LETTUCE

orange or other citrus cups furnish a wonderful variety of salad "settings." Numerous tropical, sub-tropical, and hardier fruits furnish acid and sub-acid juices for marinating or for adding the last dash to a salad that makes it "different." Florida colors in fruits—red, yellow, orange, green, with all the intervening shades, make for a strong appeal to the esthetic sense.

SPECIAL MARINADES FOR FLORIDA SALADS

Orange, lemon, lime, calamondin, sour orange juices make excellent marinades. Two parts juice to one part oil with salt to taste is the usual measure. Some fruits call for juice only. Chopped mint, parsley, pimento strips or paprika add color. Fruit juice as a marinade adds not only a flavor but food value.

D. Special Salads—Florida

Tomato With Avocado Dressing

Fresh tomato peeled and cored, and stuffed with celery. Use avocado dressing made by mashing smoothly avocado pulp into lemon or lime juice and adding a little salt. Pour over tomato. Serve on lettuce.

Avocado With Tomato Dressing

Half fresh avocado, peeled and seeded. Peel and mash fresh tomato and run through potato ricer. Season with a suggestion of tabasco. Fill cavity with dressing.

Litchi Salad

Peel and remove the seeds of litchi and stuff with a half of a Florida pecan. Serve with mayonnaise on lettuce.

Fruit Salad in Orange Cups

Three large oranges, 2 slices pineapple, diced, 12 marshmallows, quartered, $\frac{1}{3}$ cup broken nut meats, 2/3 cup strawberries, halved, lettuce.

Cut oranges into two, remove pulp carefully, leaving shell clean. Mix pineapple, marshmallows, nuts and strawberries with orange pulp. Fill orange cups, cover with cream mayonnaise and garnish with nuts. Serve on lettuce.

Grapefruit Salad

Combine grapefruit pulp with Florida grapes, stuffed with pecans; squeeze orange juice over the mixture and serve in half grapefruit hull on bed of endive. Top salad with mayonnaise (with cream).

Endive With Bacon Dressing, or Wilted Salad

Endive (or other greens) shredded. Serve with a dressing of hot bacon or fat, lemon juice and grated egg. Garnish with crisp strips of bacon. Shredded green peppers may be added.

India Salad

Grated fresh cocoanut on hearts of lettuce served with hot French dressing.

Cabbage Salad

Shred and chill $\frac{1}{2}$ small head cabbage and one white onion. Mix with half that amount of chopped celery. Dust on a little paprika. Dress with a French dressing, dashed with Worcestershire sauce. Serve in a nest of endive. Top with cubes or small slices of tomato.

Mammee Sapote Salad

Cut in half, remove seed. Add a lemon, French dressing or lemon juice, adding a few drops from a sour-sop. Serve on lettuce.

Pineapple

Shred a fresh sweet pineapple. Combine with seeded grapes and place on a nest of lettuce. Dress with mayonnaise (with cream) and top with halves of carissas.

Ponce de Leon Salad

Scoop out a little of the top heart of a Florida artichoke. Fill with a French dressing combined with chopped pimento, parsley, finely minced celery, and the mashed pulp of artichokes. Serve with a thin cheese sandwich or wafer as a course of a luncheon.

Banana and Strawberry

Make a banana boat. Combine pulp with halved strawberries and fill the boat. Use a slightly sweetened lemon dressing. Serve the banana on strawberry leaves. Serve with toasted cheese crackers and Russian tea as a luncheon.

Kumquat

Split kumquats in half lengthwise. Add seeded carissas in halves. Place a little lemon jelly in cups, fill nearly full with fruit and cover with jelly just as it begins to congeal. Set in refrigerator over night. Serve on lettuce with a cream mayonnaise mixed with crushed pecans.

Loquat-Kumquat

Slice loquats and kumquats thin. Add seeded grapes and toasted grated cocoanut. Serve on lettuce with mayonnaise.

Ambrosia Salad

Combine orange cubes, grated fresh cocoanut, cubed pineapple. Serve with a sweetened fruit dressing.

Guava Salad

Marinate guava cups in lemon juice. Fill with grated cocoanut and orange. Serve with cream mayonnaise in a lettuce nest.

Another Avocado

Fill a small half of avocado with a clear tomato jelly. Drop in a few pieces of green pepper when the tomato begins to jell. Curl lettuce leaf around each end of pear just before serving.

Sapodilla Salad

Cut fruit in half. Sprinkle with lemon or lime juice. Serve on lettuce, watercress, or other green or garnish with mint.

Florida Banana Salad

Sprinkle the fruit with lemon or lime juice. Roll in crushed peanuts. Serve on lettuce. Garnish with strawberries (with stems).

Fruit Salad Mold

Cube one grapefruit, two oranges, and one pineapple. Add four sliced kumquats and ½ cup seeded Surinam cherries. When the mold begins to set add fruit and allow to become firm. Serve in slices on lettuce with mayonnaise (with cream). If cherries are not available use grapes.

Satsuma Salad

Fill halves of satsumas with orange meat, mold with shredded pineapple and crushed pecans. Serve on lettuce with a small crystallized fig on each side.

Tangelo Salad

Cut off two inches of fruit to make a cup; mix the pulp with sliced strawberries and pecans and fill the cups. Use fruit dressing. Top with a whole strawberry.

Pineapple Salad

2 slices pineapple	French dressing
1 pineapple orange with peel	Cream cheese
1 head romaine	

Lay half slices pineapple and orange alternately on romaine. Garnish with ball of cream cheese. Serve with French dressing.

Pineapple-Fig Salad

Slice pineapple	3 pecans
Slice orange	Crystallized ginger
3 figs (preserved)	Cream mayonnaise

Place a slice of orange (with peel) on romaine and on top place a ring of green pimento. Cut figs at blossom end and press out sirup. Stuff with crystallized ginger, nuts and small pieces of orange. Place figs in pepper ring. Garnish with mayonnaise, top with pecan half or pepper chip. On each of four sides place orange slices quartered.

Perfection Salad

1 envelope gelatine (2 tablespoons)	1 cup pineapple cubes
½ cup cold water	½ cup sugar
½ cup mild vinegar	1 pimento chopped fine
1 cup boiling water	1 teaspoon salt
Juice of 1 lemon	1 cup finely shredded cabbage
1 cup celery (cut in small pieces)	

1. Add vinegar, lemon juice, sugar and salt to gelatine soaked in cold water, and dissolve in boiling water and cool.

2. Strain and when the mixture begins to set, add remaining ingredients. Turn into a mold and chill.

3. Serve on lettuce leaves with salad dressing.

E.   The Fruit and Vegetable Salad in the Menu

1. The dressing is related to the salad. Use a combination dressing with plain salad; use a plain dressing with a combined salad. Use fruit salad dressing with fruit salads.

2. If the meal is heavy use a simple acid salad.

3. Cheese combines well with fruit or vegetables for a main dish salad.

4. Avoid repeating the main ingredient of a salad in the meal.

5. Get the habit of making the fruit or raw vegetable salad the important item.

6. Remember that the salad is to be fresh, raw, chilled or crisp and attractive. Make it a habit.

4. COOKED PRODUCTS

A. Preserving the "Preventive and Protective" Value of Vegetables

The common American diet has been found to contain the following:

1. Abundance of starch, sugar and fat.

2. Adequate protein if selected properly.

3. A possible lack of vitamins, minerals and roughage.

Since the factors lacking are easily and surely supplied by vegetables, fruits and milk, it seems best to concentrate on these three groups of food in any plan of nutrition. For this reason, too, it is particularly important that we know how to preserve the minerals, roughage and vitamins in the fruits, vegetables and milk while preparing them for the family table. If we ate all of these sun-grown, soil-fed products in sufficient quantity in the fresh, natural state and without cooking, there would be no nutrition problem. That, however, would not be recommended by the most enthusiastic nutritionists. The appetite would probably not call for the quantity needed. Cooking is therefore a necessary process of preparation.

Since Florida's fruit and vegetables may be produced in abundance year in and year out in the sunshine and soil of the out-of-doors, the remaining problem is the conservation of the food value in the fruits and vegetables. Losses in the various kinds of storage and transportation are important from a nutritional viewpoint but the problem to be discussed here is that of the conservation in cooking. Food conservation is an ancient subject of interest but food value conservation belongs to the modern time.

During the past "to cook it done" has been the idea. "Water or no water," "top on or top off" has not been in the thinking. The flavor or taste has been added in the "seasoning." Texture has been simply sacrificed. Then roughage began to count; vitamins (water soluble) be-

came prominent; minerals were recognized as important and they too were being stolen away by the water. Then the cooking of fruits and vegetables became a scientific process and not just a disagreeable task.

Fresh fruit in the cooking is affected largely, as are vegetables, as to the minerals, vitamins, and roughage. Therefore the discussion at this point is limited to vegetables.

EFFECT OF HEAT ON VEGETABLES—COLOR

Children and grown-ups eat because they "like it," not because they should; because "it's good," not because "it's good for you." Attractiveness in preparation usually creates the demand. With vegetables, one of the main points of attractiveness is natural color. What is color? How is it lost? How can we retain it?

There are four color pigments in vegetables which give the natural vegetable coloring. These substances change with the action of heat, acid, and alkalis and thus change the color of the products. It is interesting to know about them.

Green (Chlorophyll)—Green vegetables, such as spinach, chard, string beans (green), green cabbage, turnip greens, carry this coloring matter or pigment which is slightly soluble in water as is shown in the cooking. Heat turns this pigment brown when there is acid present. All vegetables contain at least a trace of acid, but this acid will disappear in steam if the cover is left off the cooking vessel, and nearly all of it will go during the first fifteen minutes. If a steamer is being used the color may be improved by letting the steam escape at the end of fifteen minutes. An open kettle cooking retains better color. An alkali has the opposite effect on the "green" from that produced by the acid. A small pinch of soda has a tendency to destroy part of the vitamins and break down the fiber to a state of mush. Avoid soda. For palatability and attractiveness, then, cook "greens" by the open kettle quick method. Spinach cooks quickly, and does not lose its color. Steaming does not therefore detract.

Red (Anthocyanins)—Beets and red cabbage contain red pigment. It is very soluble in water. Alkali turns the red vegetables brown; acid turns them redder. A teaspoon of vinegar to a pint of water helps to retain color in cooking beets or red cabbage.

Colorless (Flavone)—Onions, turnips, celery and white cabbage have this pigment which is colorless until heated in the presence of alkali. Then it turns yellow. Overcooking has the same effect in onions and in cabbage.

Yellow (Carotinoid)—Carrots, squash, pumpkin and rutabaga carry this pigment, which is only slightly soluble in water and is not affected by acid or alkali. Because it is stable we need not, from the point of color, consider the cooking.

TEXTURE

Cooking softens the fiber, breaking down the natural texture. The problem is to make the product tender yet as natural as possible in texture. Spinach and okra and many other vegetables are much disliked when over-cooked. Select them tender and cook them quickly is the best plan. Again avoid the habit of adding soda to make them tender.

FLAVOR

To improve the flavor, to "season," is sometimes given as a reason for cooking vegetables instead of serving them raw. Really uncooked vegetables (mildly flavored ones) are more palatable than cooked ones and the problem is to retain the natural flavor. A few of the "strong juice" vegetables are improved with cooking, but overcooking, even of onions and cabbage, ruins the flavor and (in case of the latter) the digestibility. To preserve flavor, cook vegetables in the skin, whole, and quickly and serve at once. Potato (sweet or white), squash, pumpkin, apple, beans and other products are better when baked.

FOOD VALUE

We study tables of food value of vegetables and plan our meals. We cook the vegetables one way or another and continue to figure the food value the same. There is a big difference between cooked and uncooked vegetables from the viewpoint of minerals and vitamins. Experiments have shown that possibly from 40 to 50 per cent of the minerals and as great proportion of some vitamins dissolve into the water or are lost in cooking. Some of the minerals, at least, are in the water and should not be thrown away. Extensive experiments on many kinds of vegetables have shown that particularly cabbage, onions, and celery lose more in minerals than do other vegetables. For this reason it is a wise plan to eat raw cabbage and celery. Steamed vegetables lose less calcium than do boiled vegetables. However, greens and spinach do not lose their minerals so easily in cooking as do some others.

Phosphorus, in onions, rutabagas, and leafy vegetables, "leaks out" in cooking. Parsnips, cauliflower, and potatoes are valuable in phosphorus. Don't lose it. Bake the potatoes in their skins.

Beet greens, turnip greens and cabbage rank high in iron. The iron leaks easily, the exposed surface being great. Save the water.

Vitamins B and C are soluble in water. By saving the water we save B but C seems to be lost in the process. It seems probable that cabbage and tomatoes do not lose their C to any great extent in quick cooking. At the usual temperature there is probably only a slight loss of vitamins A and D. Vitamin E seems to be remarkably stable. Vitamin C abounds in citrus and tomatoes. They need no cooking.

THE EFFECT OF THE METHOD OF COOKING

I. Baking a vegetable in the skin preserves the food value in minerals and vitamins A and B.

1. Vegetables with high enough water content and small exposed surface, bake well. Beets, carrots, onions, parsnips, potatoes (Irish or sweet), squash, pumpkin, turnips, are good for baking.

2. Baking requires extra time and fuel.

II. Steaming is the next best method of saving food value.

1. Beets, carrots, parsnips, potato, squash and pumpkin steam well.

2. Green vegetables may be steamed but are not so attractive in color as are the open cooked "greens."

3. Steaming is more economical than baking as several vegetables may be steamed at once.

III. Steam Pressure comes third in taking care of food value.

1. Vegetables which require long time cooking are used in this method.

IV. Boiling in the Skin is rated as the fourth in methods.

1. If vegetables must be peeled, boil whole.

2. If vegetables must be cut, cut lengthwise, not crosswise, to save food value. Boiling in a large amount of water loses more minerals and vitamins than boiling in small amount. Vegetables retain flavor, texture, and food value when put on in boiling water rather than cold. Again, practically all of the minerals lost may be found in the cooking water, so do not feed the sink.

"Waterless Cooking" is comparatively new. The cooker is usually heavy aluminum, a good heat distributor. The bottom is very thick and prevents burning. The cooker may be set on the back part of a range or on a gas or oil flame. The cover fits tightly. Heat should be regulated to prevent steam escape. The cover is not removed during

FLORIDA'S FRESH VEGETABLES FOR SOUP

cooking since the method is to cook the vegetables in their own juices. Of course, strong vegetables like cabbage, Brussels sprouts, cauliflower, turnips and onions are better when they lose some of their flavor in cooking. Green vegetables become brown due to certain acids which cannot escape in a tightly closed vessel. Vegetables like potatoes (sweet and Irish) and squash and such other vegetables as are suitable for baking are suitable for waterless cooking.

VEGETABLE COOKERY

SELECTION OF VEGETABLES

1. Select usually the medium sized vegetables. Many Florida products, however, grow very quickly to a size above the average and retain their fresh tender texture and food value.

2. Select for firmness, crispness, and weight for size.

PREPARATION OF VEGETABLES FOR COOKING

1. Remove insects (if necessary) by placing the vegetable (upside down if headed) in water to which salt or vinegar has been added.

2. Wash vegetables thoroughly, using a brush. Scrape, peel, or shell after cleaning if necessary. Remember that vegetables cut crosswise lose more nutrients in cooking than vegetables cut lengthwise.

3. If it is necessary to prepare mild vegetables some time before cooking, add water to cover. When ready to cook, remove vegetables, bring water in which they have been covered to a boil and replace vegetables in this same water. Vegetables cut up and covered keep nicely in a hydrator in the refrigerator. A pan with a perforated lid serves as a substitute.

COOKING

Select the method best suited to the vegetable to be cooked taking into consideration whether texture, color, flavor summed up in attractiveness is the main item (and it sometimes is) or whether minerals and vitamins are in this particular case of more importance. Sometimes it is best to coax the appetite or desire for the cooked food and to supply the minerals and vitamins in fresh uncooked foods such as milk and fresh fruits and vegetables or their juices. Use common sense and a knowledge of the food habits of the family.

1. In boiling, put all vegetables into quickly boiling water which has been boiling long enough to drive out the air. Bring the water to a boil again as quickly as possible.

2. Start the cooking with the lid partially or entirely removed. Shove the lid off for the first three minutes of boiling of strongly flavored or of green or yellow vegetables. This gives acids and gases time to escape and leaves better flavor, color and desirability.

3. Add one teaspoon of salt to a quart of water. Add salt early in the cooking to increase color (except in red or white vegetables).

4. Use only enough water to cover mildly flavored vegetables. Let the water cook down. Do not drain. This process applies to peas, celery, string beans, lima beans.

5. Vegetables of stronger flavor (onions, cabbage, Brussels sprouts, cauliflower, turnips) should boil rapidly in larger amounts of water with open top.

6. Cook vegetables until done—no longer. Overcooking destroys color flavor, vitamins, digestibility, nutrients. Time depends upon age and tenderness of vegetables. Remove from heat as soon as tender, serve quickly with butter, with cream, with milk and butter, with white sauce or with strips of browned bacon.

7. Add no soda in cooking vegetables. It destroys vitamins, flavor and texture.

8. To follow the waterless or heavy covered aluminum saucepan method, proceed as follows:

a. Select mild flavored vegetables. Add no water, cover pan and set it over low heat. If steam escapes, lower heat.

b. For "stronger" vegetables, add a small amount of boiling water. Leave uncovered a few minutes. Cover. Use low heat.

9. To steam vegetables—

"MILD"

Select vegetables that are white, yellow or red in color (beets, wax beans, squash, potato). Spinach and some very tender greens may be steamed. For mild vegetables, choose an inset pan not perforated in bottom and lower sides but so adjusted that the steam gets to the food.

"STRONG"

For strong vegetables use a perforated pan or rack for self-draining. Allow the steam to escape some in the beginning. Place water in the bottom of the steamer. If vegetables are steamed on a perforated rack the water in the bottom will be good for soups and gravies.

10. To bake vegetables leave them in rather large pieces. Cut lengthwise in quarters—carrots, parsnips, turnips. Leave onions whole. Use a baking dish or pan. Salt, cover bottom of pan with boiling water. Cover dish or pan tightly and place in oven. In case of strong vegetables, lift the lid during the first few minutes of cooking. Use heat high enough to let the water boil—about 350 degrees. As vegetables begin to get tender, remove the cover if a fairly dry product is desired. To butter the products wait until almost all the water has evaporated. Leave the lid off and turn the heat up slightly and continue the baking until slightly brown if necessary.

B. General Recipes—Vegetables

COMMON VEGETABLE DISHES

Au Gratin—Au gratin is a French term meaning covered with crumbs. Prepare cooked vegetables as for scalloping but cover the top with buttered crumbs before browning. Sprinkle cheese over the top if desired but cheese is not essential to an au gratin dish.

Baked—Wash the vegetable and place on a pan or rack in a moderate oven. Cook until tender. Most vegetables are baked whole but squash is usually cut in pieces for serving before being baked.

Boiled—Wash the vegetable and cook it in the skin, or pared, whole or in pieces, in boiling water until just tender. The water should be boiling when the vegetable is put in and should boil continuously but not very rapidly in order not to break the vegetable. Serve with salt, pepper, and butter, or prepare in other ways such as creamed, au gratin, croquettes, or soups.

Buttered—Heat the boiled or steamed vegetable in butter or pour melted butter over the hot cooked vegetable.

Creamed—Combine the cooked vegetable whole or in pieces with white sauce. The usual proportions are one cup of vegetables to one cup of white sauce. For moist vegetables, such as carrots, turnips or onions, use medium white sauce. For dry vegetables, like potatoes, use thin white sauce.

Cream Soups—Combine a mashed or strained cooked vegetable with thin white sauce. The usual proportions are one cup of vegetable to two cups of sauce.

Croquettes—Combine a mashed or finely diced cooked vegetable with thick white sauce. Shape into individual servings of the desired form, roll in crumbs, in beaten egg, and in crumbs again, and fry in deep fat.

Curried—Add curry powder to white sauce and prepare as for creamed vegetable.

Scalloped (cooked)—Cut cooked vegetables or a combination of vegetables in slices or pieces, combine with white sauce as for creamed vegetable, put into a buttered baking dish, and brown in the oven.

Scalloped (raw)—Put a layer of the sliced raw vegetable in the bottom of a buttered baking dish, sprinkle with flour, salt, and pepper, and dot with butter. Repeat the layers until the dish is full and pour over the top just enough milk to be seen through the top layer. Bake in a moderate oven until the vegetable is tender.

Jerusalem Artichoke

Wash and pare and cook one quart of artichokes in boiling salt water until soft. Add ¼ cup butter, 2 tablespoons lemon juice, 2 teaspoons salt, and a few grains cayenne. Cook 3 minutes and serve hot.

ASPARAGUS

Cut off lower parts of stalks as far down as they will snap. The end of the stalk may be cut in pieces and cooked until tender and served as creamed or scalloped asparagus or used as a puree in stock or cream soups.

To avoid overcooking the tips, after scraping off any tiny leaves, wash the asparagus, cut it into equal lengths, discard the tough portions, tie it in bunches with a soft string, and cook it standing upright in a deep saucepan. The water should come about two-thirds of the way to the tips, which should be cooked by the steam alone. Cook until tender but not soft. As with most green vegetables, asparagus is better slightly undercooked than overcooked. Serve the asparagus in long or short pieces, on buttered toast with melted butter or a cream sauce.

Scalloped Asparagus

2 cups milk	Salt and pepper
2 tablespoons butter	2 eggs, yolks
2 tablespoons flour	1 cup buttered bread crumbs
2 bunches (about 1 quart) of asparagus	

Make a thin white sauce and add the cooked asparagus. Add the beaten yolks and turn the mixture into buttered baking dish. Cover with buttered crumbs and brown in a moderate over (350°-400° F.).

Buttered Crumbs—To each cup of ground crumbs, use 3 tablespoons of butter or other fat. Melt the fat, add the crumbs, remove them from the heat and mix them thoroughly until each crumb is coated with fat. This mixture browns easily and gives a delicious flavor to a creamed dish.

Asparagus Shells

1 cup asparagus puree	1 teaspoon salt
2 cups hot mashed potatoes	½ cup fine dry bread crumbs
1 egg	

Mix the asparagus, potato, salt and beaten egg thoroughly. On a well-greased baking sheet, shape the mixture into small circular forms with a hollow center. Brush the entire surface with melted butter, sprinkle lightly with bread crumbs, and set in a hot oven (400°-450° F.) until thoroughly heated and golden brown. With a broad spatula or pancake turner lift the shells to a hot platter. Fiil them with diced cream chicken or mushrooms. Serve at once.

BANANA

Banana may be used in any number of dessert combinations with eggs, milk, sugar and starch. It is best baked simply with the addition of lemon or orange juice and a little salt. There is enough fat and also of sugar without the use of more.

LIMA BEANS

Cook young lima beans in BOILING salted water until tender, allowing water to cook quite low. Moisten well with thin cream or butter, salt and pepper.

Succotash

2 cups fresh corn	2 tablespoons butter
1 cup lima beans	Salt, pepper
½ cup milk	

Boil beans until tender. Add corn and cook 10 minutes. Add milk, butter, salt and pepper. Cook 3 minutes longer.

Creole Lima Beans

1½ cups dried lima beans	1 small onion
2 tablespoons butter or other cooking fat	1½ tablespoons flour
2 tablespoons chopped green pepper	1 teaspoon sugar
1 cup canned or stewed tomato	½ teaspoon salt

Soak the beans overnight and cook until tender. Heat the butter and cook the chopped pepper and onion in it for a few minutes. Add flour and blend thoroughly. Add the tomato gradually and cook until thickened, stirring constantly. Add seasoning, pour over the beans and cook 15 minutes.

Lima Beans, French Style

1 cup dried lima beans	½ teaspoon salt
1½ cups milk	2 egg yolks
4 tablespoons butter	

Soak the beans overnight and cook until almost done, using no more water than the beans will absorb. Add milk, butter and salt, and finish cooking. Just before serving stir in the beaten egg yolks and cook until slightly thickened.

STRING BEANS

Select tender beans. String well. Drop into boiling salted water and cook until tender, being careful to see that the water evaporates as the beans are done. Brown strips of bacon in a pan. Add bacon and drippings to beans and allow them to cook a few minutes longer until well seasoned.

Succotash (String Beans)

Cook beans as for boiling and add in proportion of one cup of each grated corn and stewed tomato and cook until well combined (about ten minutes).

BEETS
Buttered Beets

Leave on the skin, end of the root, and 2 inches of the stem. Wash the beets and boil them until they are tender. Take them from the boiling water and drop into cold water. Slip off the skin, cut the beets in thin slices or dice them. Heat them with salt, pepper and butter and serve at once.

VARIATION—To each pint of hot buttered beets add from 1 to 2 tablespoons of vinegar or lemon juice, 1 teaspoon of sugar, and 1 tablespoon of minced green pepper.

Beet Greens

Examine the leaves carefully, rejecting all bruised or dark portions. Do not separate the roots from the leaves. Wash thoroughly in many waters. Add only enough boiling water to keep the beets from burning, and boil until tender, from 20 to 30 minutes. Drain off the water, cut off the ends of the roots and peel the beets. Chop the greens slightly and season with butter, salt and pepper.

Harvard Beets

Cook as for buttered beets. Mix ½ cup sugar and ½ tablespoon cornstarch. Add ½ cup vinegar and let boil 5 minutes. Add beets and let stand on back of range 30 minutes. Just before serving add 2 tablespoons butter.

BRUSSELS SPROUTS

Cook in boiling salted water about 20 minutes or until tender. Drain. Add butter or cream.

Brussels Sprouts With Celery

Chop 1 quart sprouts as above. Chop celery, 1½ cups and cook two minutes in 3 tablespoons butter. Add 2 tablespoons flour and pour on gradually 1½ cups scalded milk. Bring to a boil. Add sprouts, season with salt and pepper, and, as soon as heated, serve.

BROCCOLI

To preserve the attractive texture and flower of the Broccoli, arrange with "heads up" in a vessel. Steam in salted water for a few minutes with the vessel open to preserve the green color. Cook until tender. Season with butter or bacon fat or with a combination of butter and bacon.

CABBAGE

Chop or shred cabbage and cook in uncovered vessel in boiling salted water. Cabbage may be overcooked very easily. Remove as soon as tender. Add butter or cream. Cabbage is of fine flavor when boiled in water in which ham (especially a ham bone) has been boiled.

Boiled Cabbage

Cabbage being among the "strong" vegetables is cooked in a generous amount of water and with the top open for at least fifteen minutes. Season with ham or with butter, salt and pepper. Cook only until tender.

Cabbage Rolls

2 cups mashed potatoes	Celery salt
1 medium-sized onion	Cabbage leaves
1 green pepper or pimento	Boiling water or stock
Salt and pepper	Sage to taste
1 cup cold cooked meat, ground or chopped	

Combine the vegetables, meat and seasonings, and shape the mixture into small rolls. Roll each of these in a wilted cabbage leaf (wilted by placing in boiling water for 5 minutes) and place them in a greased baking dish. Add sufficient boiling water or stock to cover them about halfway. Cover and bake in a moderate oven until the cabbage leaves are tender.

CHINESE CABBAGE

Use raw or cooked. This cabbage requires even less cooking than common cabbage. The inside leaves are better uncooked. (See Salads.)

CAULIFLOWER

Remove the green and imperfect leaves from the cauliflower and place it top downward in a dish of cold salted water to draw out the dust and other impurities. Leave whole or break into flowers, boil until tender in a large amount of water and serve with salt, pepper and butter.

CAULIFLOWER

Cauliflower, French Style

1 cauliflower	4 tablespoons flour
2 quarts water	⅜ pound sorrel or endive
2 tablespoons salt	2 tablespoons cream
5 tablespoons butter	1 egg yolk

Boil the cauliflower for twenty minutes in the salt water. Cook the finely chopped sorrel for ten minutes. Make a white sauce of the flour and part of the butter and the juice of the vegetables.

Put the cauliflower through a sieve—return to the soup—add the white sauce and, just before serving, add the well-mixed egg yolk and cream.

Cauliflower Loaf

1 large cauliflower	4 tablespoons butter
3 tablespoons flour	3 tablespoons cream
1 cup milk	8 eggs

Cook the cauliflower until tender in boiling salt water, drain well; rub through a sieve.

Make a cream sauce with the flour, butter, cream and milk. Mix with the cauliflower and add the egg yolks and lastly fold in the stiffly beaten whites. Put in a buttered mold, set in water—cook covered for at least 1 hour. Ten minutes before serving, remove the cover and brown. Turn it out of the mold and serve with tomato sauce. (French Selected.)

Cauliflower Au Gratin

1 medium-sized cauliflower	Salt and paprika
1½ cups thin white sauce	Buttered crumbs
2/3 cup cheese	

When the white sauce is smooth, add the cheese, the salt and the paprika, and pour the sauce over the cooked cauliflower. Turn the mixture into a buttered baking dish. Cover with buttered crumbs. Brown in a moderate over (350°-400° F.) from 15 to 20 minutes.

Cauliflower With Cheese Sauce

1 medium-sized cauliflower	4 tablespoons grated cheese
1½ cups thin white sauce	Salt and paprika

Add the cheese to the smooth white sauce and pour it over the cooked cauliflower just before serving.

KOHL-RABI

Select small bulbs having crisp new leaves. Cut leaves and bulbs in small pieces. Boil the bulb in salted water for 15 minutes, then add leaves and cook an additional 30 minutes. Slice the bulb, arrange the greens around the edge of the dish and place the slices in the center. Season with melted butter.

RAPE

Cook rape according to other tender greens by the open kettle boiling method. Cook quickly.

RAPE

CARROTS

Wash and scrape young carrots. Boil or steam until tender. Add butter, pepper, salt to taste. Add cream sauce if desired or use only butter. Carrots may be boiled with meat. They may be used whole for garnish, around the meat platter.

Carrot Soup

1 pint milk	1 tablespoon onion juice
1 cup cooked carrot, pressed through a strainer	1 tablespoon minced parsley, celery or celery salt
2 tablespoons butter	

Heat the milk, combine the other ingredients, heat them, and add them to the heated milk.

Stuffed Carrots

4 carrots	1 cup cooked rice
1/3 cup ground boiled ham	1 tablespoon butter
Salt	Pepper
1/4 teaspoon celery salt	Buttered bread crumbs

Scrub the carrots and cook them until tender. Remove the skins, cut off the root end, and split the carrots in half lengthwise. Combine the other ingredients and mix thoroughly. Pile the stuffing on the carrot halves, sprinkle with the buttered crumbs, and brown in a moderate oven.

Carrot Souffle

1 cup carrots, boiled and mashed	2 eggs
1 tablespoon minced onion	Salt and paprika
1 cup medium white sauce	

Add the carrot, the onion and the seasoning to the white sauce, then add the beaten egg yolks. Beat the whites of the eggs until they are stiff. Fold them lightly into the first mixture, and turn this into a buttered baking dish. Set the dish in a pan of hot water and bake the souffle' in a moderate oven (350°-400° F.) for 30 minutes. Serve it at once.

Carrots and Peas

Boil whole. Cut in cubes. Combine with equal quantity of cooked green peas. Season with butter or light cream, salt and pepper.

Carrots Lyonnaise

2 cups carrots cut into thin strips	2 tablespoons butter
2 teaspoons chopped onion	1 tablespoon chopped parsley
Salt and pepper	

Boil carrots ten minutes and drain. Melt butter, add onion and cook five minutes. Then add carrots and salt and pepper to season. Stir gently until well blended. Pile in hot dish and sprinkle with parsley.

Creamed Carrots With Peanut Butter

6 carrots	1 cup white sauce (medium)	1 tablespoon peanut butter

Dice the carrots and cook until soft. Make white sauce, adding to it the peanut butter. Pour over the carrots and serve hot.

Carrot Relish

1 quart carrots, ground	1 pint vinegar
1 cup celery, chopped fine	1/2 cup sugar
1 large red or green pepper, chopped	2 teaspoons salt
1 medium sized onion, chopped	1/2 teaspoon paprika

Cook carrot until tender. Chop celery and other ingredients very fine. Combine ingredients and cook until mixture is clear.

Carrot Chutney

RED PART	YELLOW PART
2 pounds of sweet Spanish pimento or No. 1 cans of pimento	1 pint of small carrots, sliced. Cook until tender
1 pound of sugar	½ pint of gingered watermelon rind
Juice of 4 lemons	
2 hot peppers	

Red Part—Place sweet peppers in a hot oven, blister and peel. Chop sweet and hot pepper together, add sugar and lemon juice, and let stand in an enameled vessel or crock for 5 hours. Drain off the liquor and allow it to simmer for ten minutes. Pour it over the peppers again and let stand for 2 hours. Simmer the liquor again for fifteen minutes, allowing the peppers to remain in while simmering.

Yellow Part—Use one pint of sliced carrots (cooked) and one-half pint gingered watermelon rind chopped or cut into small uniform pieces.

Packing—A ten-ounce jar is an attractive package for this product. In packing, place the heavier color—red—at the bottom in a one-inch layer; then place a one-inch layer of yellow. Continue in this manner until the jar is nearly filled. Combine the liquors and boil five minutes, strain, and pour over the contents. Paddle to remove air bubbles. Cap, clamp, and process for ten minutes.

Glazed Carrots

6 carrots (medium size)
2/3 cup brown sugar
½ cup water
2 tablespoons butter

Clean and cook whole carrots in small amount of salt water. Make a sirup of the brown sugar, water and butter. Place cooked carrots in sirup in a heavy frying pan. Baste carrots until they have a rich glaze. Serve with roast meat.

Carrot and Apple Pie

1 cup grated carrots
1 cup diced tart apples
1 cup sugar
⅓ cup raisins
1 cup grated pineapple
1 tablespoon butter
½ cup water
Nutmeg and vanilla

CHANTENAY CARROTS

Cook carrot, apple, pineapple together. Make sirup of sugar and water. Add raisins and cook until tender and plump. Combine all and cook the mixture, with the exception of the butter and the seasoning, until it is thick and clear. Remove from heat. Beat in one egg, add butter and seasoning. Turn it into a crust that has been baked, and cover it with meringue. Bake it in a slow oven for 25 minutes.

Carrot Dessert

Grated carrot	Cocoanut
Pineapple	Whipped cream

Orange and Carrot Marmalade

6 carrots, medium size
3 oranges

1 lemon, juice and grated rind
Sugar

Dice the carrots and cook them until they are tender, in as little water as possible. Cut the oranges and the lemon in small pieces. Measure the carrot and fruit, and add 2/3 as much sugar. Simmer the mixture until it is clear. Turn it into jelly glasses, and when it is cold, seal it with paraffin.

Carrot Custard

2 eggs
½ cup milk
¼ cup fine bread crumbs

½ teaspoon salt
1 tablespoon melted butter
1½ cups grated raw carrot

Beat eggs slightly and add remaining ingredients. Turn into greased custard cups, place in steamer basket, set over boiling water, cover and cook until the custard is firm, about 30 minutes. Unmold and serve as a vegetable or with cheese or egg sauce as a main course at luncheon or supper.

CASSAVA PUDDING

One level cup grated cassava, ½ cup milk, 1¾ cups sugar, 1 egg, 1 teaspoon salt, 4½ cups water, 1 tablespoon butter, flavor with nutmeg. Bake 1 hour.

CELERY

The coarse outside stalks may be used for cooking, reserving the tender hearts for salads, sandwiches, and eating raw.

CELERY

Scalloped Celery

2 cups cooked celery, cut in pieces
1 cup medium white sauce
1 tablespoon finely minced onion

3 tablespoons grated cheese
Buttered bread crumbs
Salt and pepper

Put the celery into a greased baking dish. Add the cheese to the white sauce, flavored with onion, and pour it over the celery. Cover with the buttered crumbs and bake in a moderate oven until golden brown.

Stewed Celery

1 pint celery, cut into 1-inch pieces
2 tablespoons flour
2 tablespoons butter

½ cup milk
Salt and pepper

Cook the celery until tender. Make a medium white sauce of the celery water, milk, flour and butter. Add the cooked celery to the white sauce and season to taste with salt and pepper.

Celery Flavor

Celery (chopped) may be added to an oyster omelet or scrambled egg and oyster combination. It should be cooked only partially and should be crisp. It gives a nice "crunchy feel" to an otherwise soft dish.

Celery Raw

The best recipe for celery is as follows: Clean well. Crisp. Serve.

Celery Relish

2 quarts celery or six bunches
3 quarts cabbage or 2 large heads

1 quart onions

Chop and cover with salt water for two days. Drain well and put on stove with:

1½ quarts vinegar
¼ pound mustard
1 tablespoon tumeric powder

4 cups brown sugar
1 tablespoon flour

Boil twenty minutes, then add three well-beaten eggs before taking from heat. Add more salt and sugar if needed.

American Chop Suey

1 pound round steak ground
1 cup raw rice
1 green pepper (cut fine)
1 large onion

1 large bunch celery
1 pint tomatoes
1 can mushrooms may be added

Brown meat slightly in small quantity of fat, add all other ingredients which have been cut. Cook until vegetables are tender.

CHILI CON CARNE

One pound hamburger, one-half can pimentos, cut fine; two large onions, cut fine; one cup diced celery, one teaspoon sugar, one pint tomatoes, one package spaghetti, cooked in boiling salted water. When spaghetti is tender, drain off water; add hamburger, celery, tomatoes, pimentos, onions, sugar. Cook slowly until meat is done. Add salt and pepper to taste.

CELERY CHOWDER

4 cupfuls finely diced celery
3 large potatoes, diced
1 medium sized onion, chopped
2 tablespoonfuls flour

1½ teaspoonfuls salt
⅛ teaspoonful pepper
1 quart milk
2 hard cooked eggs

Melt the fat in a kettle. Then add the chopped onion, celery and potatoes. Cover with boiling water and simmer gently until the celery and potatoes are tender. Then add the salt, pepper, and milk. Heat well and thicken with the flour which has been rubbed smooth in two tablespoonfuls of water. Just before serving add the hard-cooked eggs chopped. Serve with crackers.

SWISS CHARD

Cook like spinach in a small amount of water. Stir until it settles in the water.

COLLARDS

Select tender leaves after frost (if in frost section). Cook until tender in a generous amount of water to evaporate as the greens become quite tender. Season with cured bacon or ham hock. Usually the meat (with bone) is placed in cold water and allowed to come to a boil and cook for a while before the greens are added. Add salt to taste after greens have cooked for a while. Chop fine. Serve with a sour relish or pickle.

SWEET CORN
(On the cob)

Select sound ears of green corn. Husk and silk. Cook immediately in boiling salted water 10 to 12 minutes. Serve at once with butter.

SUCCOTASH
(See Lima Beans)

1 pint shelled lima beans	3 tablespoons butter
3 cups green corn	Salt and pepper

Cook the beans until tender in just enough water to cover them. Add the corn and cook for 15 minutes longer. Season with butter, salt and pepper, and serve. The succotash may be made from canned corn and beans.

VEGETABLE SOUP MIXTURE
(Canned for out-of-season)

This should be made in the proportion of one-half tomato pulp, one-fourth corn or tiny lima beans, and one-fourth okra, with seasoning added. One slice of onion should be added to each No. 2 can. The tomatoes should be heated, rubbed through a sieve, and cooked down to about the consistency of ketchup before measuring; then the corn, okra, onion and seasoning should be added and cooked until the corn and okra are about three-fourths done. Then pack into cans and process one hour at boiling, or 25 minutes at 10 pounds steam pressure.

CORN AND TOMATO CHOWDER

2 cups canned corn	1 cup milk
1 cup canned or ripe tomatoes	½ cup grated cheese
2 cups diced celery	½ cup chopped pimentos
1 quart cold water	3 tablespoons flour
2 tablespoons butter	2 teaspoons salt

Place corn, tomatoes, diced celery, and one teaspoonful salt in a kettle and cover with cold water. Boil ½ hour. Melt fat and add flour gradually. Then add the cold milk, stirring constantly. Add the vegetable mixture gradually to the white sauce; add seasonings. Add to the chowder the grated cheese and pimentos, chopped fine. Stir until cheese is melted. Serve piping hot. A cream soup may be made, if desired, by straining out the vegetables before adding the white sauce. Serves six to eight.

CORN PUDDING

To two cups grated or chopped corn add two eggs, slightly beaten, 2 tablespoons melted butter and one pint scalded milk; turn into buttered baking dish and bake in a slow oven.

ROAST CORN

Build a camp fire and allow to burn to a bed of coals and hot ashes. Place ears of green corn in husks (all except outermost leaves) in hot ashes with coals. Cook until tender. Serve immediately with butter and salt. American Indians packed the ears of corn in clay and roasted them.

CORN MEAL

Southern corn meal (home ground) contains more of the food value and natural flavor of the original product than does the finely "bolted" meal. It is, therefore, a very popular food product. Any corn meal dish requires thorough cooking and a high temperature to bring out the nutty flavor and to thoroughly cook the starch. Because the corn dishes are used so extensively with vegetables in the South, the following recipes are given:

Corn Muffins or Breadsticks

2 cups meal	1 teaspoon baking powder
1 teaspoon salt	2 cups buttermilk
½ teaspoon soda	2 eggs
3 tablespoons lard or bacon grease or butter	

Mix all ingredients. Add one tablespoon cane sirup if desired. Add melted lard last. Pour into hot greased muffin rings or iron breadstick molds. Cook in very hot oven 30 minutes.

Corn Meal Batter Bread

Use same recipe for muffins. Combine. Pour into hot, greased skillet and cook in hot oven from 30 to 40 minutes, depending upon thickness of loaf.

Hoecake

Corn meal—water—salt. Place iron or aluminum griddle over heat. Grease well and allow to get piping hot. Pour hot water over corn meal and salt and mix thoroughly. Place on hot griddle and pat out to "fit." When the hoecake is well browned, turn on a plate or on your hand, if experienced. After turning, cover so as to hold some of the steam. When both sides are well browned, allow to cook more slowly until well done.

Corn Dodger

Corn dodger is made like hoecake except a little butter or lard is added. It is formed into small pones about three inches long and dropped into the quickly boiling water in the vessels where turnip greens, peas, or collards are cooking. About twenty minutes or more should be allowed for cooking. They are served with the vegetable. In this way the cooking water is preserved in the menu. A most tasty article of food is the corn dodger.

Indian Pudding

5 cups milk	1 teaspoon salt
⅓ cup corn meal	1 teaspoon ginger
½ cup molasses	

Cook milk and meal in a double boiler for twenty minutes; add molasses, salt and ginger; pour into a buttered pudding dish and bake two hours in a slow oven; serve with cream.

Corn Meal and Fig Pudding

1 cup corn meal	1 cup finely chopped figs
1 cup molasses	2 eggs
6 cups milk (or 4 of milk and 2 of cream)	1 teaspoon salt

Cook the corn meal with four cups of milk in a double boiler for twenty minutes; add the figs and salt. When the mixture is cool, add the eggs well beaten. Pour into a buttered pudding dish and bake in a moderate oven for three hours or more. When partly cooked, add the remainder of the milk without stirring the pudding. Fig preserves may be substituted for the dried figs. Drain the figs from sirup and slightly dry in the oven before using.

CUCUMBERS

Cucumbers should be served raw. See Relishes and Pickles. They may be steamed and buttered like squash.

EGGPLANT

2 small eggplants	Salt and pepper
1/4 cup oil	1/2 tablespoon flour
1 1/2 tablespoons butter	1 tablespoon water
1 1/2 pounds tomatoes	Bouquet powder
1 onion	

Peel the eggplants and cut into 1/2-inch slices, sprinkle lightly with salt, and let stand covered with a cloth. After 1 hour, drain and dry them carefully. Brown in the oil and drain.

For the other part prepare a tomato sauce by cooking the tomatoes and onions, cut into pieces, with the butter, salt, pepper and bouquet; cook until thick and strain.

Put the eggplant in a pan with alternate layers of tomato sauce. Put bits of butter on top and bake for twenty minutes.

Eggplant

Slice and pare the eggplant. Place the slices in a buttered baking dish, add salt and bits of butter and sprinkle generously with grated cheese. Cover with sliced tomatoes, add salt, pepper and butter. Bake in a moderate oven until the eggplant is tender, from 30 to 45 minutes.

Sauteed Eggplant

Peel the eggplant and cut it into one-half inch slices. Sprinkle each slice with salt. Pile the slices in a bowl and place a plate on top to weight them down slightly. Let stand for two hours. The salt will draw out any disagreeable flavor. Wipe each slice dry, dip it in crumbs, in beaten egg, and in crumbs again, and saute' slowly in hot fat.

Eggplant Scallop

Slice the eggplant, but do not pare it. Saute' the slices in butter, bacon fat or drippings. Arrange the slices in a baking dish in layers with a sprinkling of cheese between layers. When the dish is about three-fourths full, cover the eggplant with a medium white sauce. Cover the top with buttered crumbs and bake in a moderate oven until brown.

ENDIVE

Endive is used largely for salads. A wilted salad is made by using hot bacon grease instead of oil in the dressing. This adds a good flavor. Sliced or grated hard cooked egg combines nicley as to color and food combination. Endive should be chopped fine. Boiled salad dressing may be added to bacon. Escarole, Romaine, water cress, lettuce (green) may be prepared in the same way or may be used as cooked "greens."

KALE

CURLY ENDIVE

4 heads chicory (curly endive)
1 tablespoon meat broth or cream
1 tablespoon butter
3 1/2 tablespoons butter
1/3 cup croutons

Wash the endive thoroughly and cook in boiling salted water without covering. When it is tender, drain and rinse and chop fine. Put in a pan with the butter, salt, pepper, stock or cream and heat through. Decorate the dish in which it is served with croutons of bread browned in butter.

CURLY MUSTARD GREEN MUSTARD

GREENS

Leeks, spinach, mustard, kale, radish, turnip greens may be used in any of the recipes for greens. Examine all greens and wash them carefully, discarding any wilted or yellow leaves. Leave the roots on for the first washing as this makes the greens easier to handle; then cut them off to allow a more thorough cleansing. Wash in at least 3 waters, lifting the greens out of the pan before emptying the water so that the sand and other impurities will be left in the bottom of the pan.

Greens may be cooked quickly in a large amount of water or for a slightly longer time in a small amount of water. Cook until just tender and no longer. Serve with salt, pepper, and butter, or season with bacon while cooking. Hard cooked eggs may always be used with any of these "greens."

OKRA

Okra is used in a number of combination dishes with tomatoes, corn or lima beans. It is often cooked with field peas by dropping the tender pods into the vessel with the peas when they are nearly cooked. The steam from the peas will cook the okra. The combination, with a few slices of fresh tomato or sweet green peppers, makes a splendid vegetable plate. Plain, steamed or boiled okra should be whole and unbroken.

Okra Gumbo

The real Creole gumbo is made as follows: Wash one-half gallon of okra pods, dry on a towel; cut off ends of pods, and slice. Put one-third cup of lard and two tablespoons of minced onion into a kettle and fry a young chicken, previously jointed, until a golden brown. Remove chicken, add the sliced okra and one small chopped tomato. Fry until no more "strings" come from the okra. Then put the chicken in and salt and pepper to taste. Add one quart of boiling water. Cook three-fourths hour. Serve in soup plates with a portion of boiled rice in each plate. When chicken cannot be secured, use ham.

ONIONS

Bermuda onions are mild flavored. Place onions under water to peel. Boil in plenty of water, drain, and again cover with boiling salted water. Cook until soft but not broken. Drain. Add a little milk or cream. Cook a few minutes. Season with butter.

Glazed Onions

After boiling 15 minutes small silverskin onions, drain and dry. Melt 3 tablespoons butter, add 2 tablespoons sugar and onions and cook until browned. An asbestos mat is needed under the vessel during last few minutes.

LEEKS OR GREEN ONIONS

Leeks Au Gratin

12 leeks	1 cup grated cheese
6 potatoes	Buttered bread crumbs
1 cup medium white sauce	Salt and pepper

Cook the leeks in boiling water until tender. Boil, pare, and slice the potatoes. Arrange the vegetables in alternate layers in a buttered baking dish and pour the white sauce over them. Add the cheese, the buttered bread crumbs, and the seasoning, and bake for 15 minutes in a moderate oven.

Onions Au Gratin

6 medium-sized onions	Salt and pepper
¼ cup grated cheese	Stock or hot water
½ cup toasted bread crumbs	2 tablespoons melted butter

Boil the onions until slightly tender and remove the centers with an apple corer. Fill the cavities with the cheese and crumbs mixed together. Place the onions in a baking dish. Add ½ cup of the stock in which onions were boiled, salt and pepper, dot with butter, and bake in a moderate oven until brown.

Scalloped Onions and Peanuts

Cut the onions in quarters; cook them in salted boiling water until tender. Add salt just before the cooking is completed. Drain them and save the broth for soup. Butter a baking dish. Put into it a layer of onions, and sprinkle over them some ground peanuts; add another layer of onions and peanuts. Pour over all the cream. Cover the top with buttered crumbs and brown the dish in the oven. Any vegetable may be scalloped in this way. Cheese may be used in place of peanuts if desired, or grated cheese may be combined with the cream.

Stuffed Onions

Cook medium-sized onions in boiling salted water for 15 minutes. Drain, and remove the centers, leaving a shell about one-half inch thick. Make a stuffing of equal parts of chopped cold meat and bread crumbs or rice. Moisten the mixture with stock or tomato juice and season with salt and pepper. Fill the onion shells with the mixture and put them in the oven to brown for 15 minutes.

PARSNIPS

The simplest method of cooking parsnips is to wash them clean, boil them, and then scrape off the skin. Slice or chop them coarsely and season with salt and butter.

Breaded Parsnips

Boil rather large parsnips until tender, and scrape off their skin. Cut the parsnips crosswise in slices about one-third inch thick. Season the slices with salt and pepper. Dip each slice in beaten egg and then in fine bread crumbs. Fry in deep fat, drain on soft paper, and serve as a border for meat platter.

PEAS

Green Peas

Cook in boiling salted water until tender, allowing water to evaporate. Add milk, butter, pepper and salt to season.

Scalloped Cow Peas

1 cup dried cow peas	1 tablespoon sugar
½ cup uncooked rice	1 tablespoon butter
¼ cup chopped onion	Salt, pepper
1½ cups canned or stewed tomatoes	

Soak the peas over night and cook until almost done, using no more water than the peas will absorb. Add the remaining ingredients and continue cooking until the peas and rice are tender.

Field Peas

Field peas require a longer period for cooking.

Green Peas (Little Peas), French Style

1 pound peas
  Some young onions
6 tablespoons butter

1 head lettuce
  A sprig of parsley
1 egg yolk

Sauté the peas in a pan with the butter. Add the lettuce, which has been washed and tied in a bunch, onions, parsley, salt, pepper and little sugar. Shake the pan until well mixed. Add a cup water; cover and cook on a slow fire 1½ hours. A little before serving remove the parsley; add the rest of the butter and an egg yolk.

PEPPERS—SWEET

Peppers, used largely for raw salads, relishes and decorations, have become popular as stuffed dishes. They add a delightful flavor to the dressing and make new dishes of "left-overs."

Stuffed Peppers

6 medium sized green peppers
2 medium slices or 1½ lb. smoked ham
2 eggs
½ teaspoon salt

1 cup canned tomatoes
½ cup cracker crumbs
1 very small onion
Few sprigs parsley

Simmer ham in 1 cup boiling water 5 minutes. Drain, reserving the liquid. Put the ham through a meat chopper; mix with the tomatoes, cracker crumbs and the eggs well beaten. Chop the onion and parsley very fine and add to the mixture. Wash the peppers and remove the seeds. Fill the pepper shells with the mixture and place them in shallow baking dish surrounded by the water in which the ham was simmered.

SWEET POTATO
Baked

Sweet potato develops the best flavor when baked. Wash well, grease with butter or bacon and bake in covered pan inside oven. The skin when brown cracks and allows steam to escape. Split through center or break into halves crosswise and butter. Serve hot. A *good* sweet potato needs no extra "trimmings."

Potatoes Baked on Half Shell

Bake potatoes, cut lengthwise, remove contents, mash, season with sugar and butter and salt. (Peanuts or pecans may be added). Place in potato shells, cover with marshmallows and brown.

Sweet Potato and Peanut Croquettes

1 cup mashed sweet potato
1 egg
1 tablespoon flour
1 cup finely ground parched peanuts or pecans

½ teaspoon salt
Cayenne pepper
Bread crumbs

Combine the ingredients, and shape the mixture into croquettes. Roll them in bread crumbs, beaten egg, and crumbs again. Fry them in deep fat.

Potato Pone

1 quart grated raw sweet potatoes
1 egg
3 tablespoons butter, melted
1 cup milk
1 teaspoon cinnamon

¾ cup cane sirup
½ cup flour
½ teaspoon nutmeg
¾ teaspoon salt

Sift together the dry ingredients. Combine these with the remaining ingredients. Put the mixture in a baking dish and bake it in a slow oven about two and one-half hours, or until done, stirring occasionally during the first of the cooking. During the last thirty minutes, discontinue the stirring and allow the pone to brown. Many people prefer to serve the dish cold with milk or cream. When cold it can be sliced. It is frequently served hot, as a vegetable.—Sarah W. Partridge.

Sweet Potato Tournado

Select potatoes about two inches in diameter. Cook them in boiling water until tender. Peel and cut in pieces two inches long. Around each piece wrap a thin slice of bacon and fasten with toothpick. Place on a pan in a hot oven until the bacon is crisp. Serve with parsley garnish.

Breaded Sweet Potatoes

Peel boiled sweet potatoes and cut them in lengthwise slices. Dip the slices in beaten egg, then in crumbs, and fry in deep fat. Drain on soft paper. Serve hot.

Candied Potatoes

4 medium potatoes	¼ cup butter
1 cup water	1½ cup sugar
1 teaspoon salt	¼ cup vinegar or lemon juice
1 teaspoon cinnamon	

Cut uncooked sweet potato into slices, then strips about ⅓ inch thick. Place in a baking dish. Add butter and sprinkle with sugar. Pour on water. Dash with cinnamon. Add vinegar. Bake until sugar and butter are candied and the potatoes are well cooked. Lemon juice may be substituted for vinegar.

Ash Roast
(Out-door Cookery)

This old-fashioned method of cooking sweet potatoes develops their finest flavor and one unapproached through any other method. Select and wash smooth, uniform potatoes of medium size. Make a bed of them in the hot ashes of a burning fire. Cover well with the ashes, over this bank glowing coals. Roast the potatoes until soft throughout. When soft, remove from the ashes, peel and serve. They should be eaten hot with butter. This method is especially adapted to the open fireplace or to camp cookery and is frequently used at the time of sirup and sugar making on the farm when the hot ashes and glowing coals at the entrance of the furnace suggest it. It may be practiced on a wood stove, utilizing the hot ashes in the ash pan as a bed for the potatoes and covering them with a layer of glowing coals.—Sarah W. Partridge.

WHITE POTATO

White potatoes are more generally used as bread. Baked and boiled in the jackets are the best methods. Butter, milk, cream or cheese add the needed flavor and seasoning. Parsley, a contrasting color, adds attractiveness as well as flavor to the potato.

Potato, with a starch content of 18 to 20 per cent, is usually "mealy" when cooked. Mealy potatoes are best for baking, boiling or deep frying. Potatoes. containing more protein and less starch are "waxy" and better for salad, scalloping and creaming because they retain their shape. A light, sandy soil usually produces a larger starch content than heavy soil. Both young potatoes and stored potatoes have more cellulose in proportion to starch than have fresh matured potatoes.

Baked Potato

Select potatoes of uniform size; scrub them with vegetable brush; place them on a grate or in a pan in a hot oven and bake them for 45 minutes, or until they are tender. If they are overcooked, they will be soggy rather than mealy. Crack or pierce the skin as soon as the potatoes are done to let out the steam which otherwise will condense and make the potatoes soggy.

Boiled Potatoes

Drop well-washed potatoes into boiling salted water. Cook them, with the cover of the kettle ajar, just until they are tender, about 20 to 30 minutes. Drain off the water immediately, cover them with a cloth which will absorb the moisture, and place them where they will keep warm. Overcooking and standing in water makes a soggy, unpalatable potato.

Steamed Potatoes

Prepare the potatoes as for boiling, place them in a steamer, cover them tight, and steam them for about 30 minutes, or until just tender. Remove the skins and serve the potato at once.

Stuffed Potatoes

Cut baked potatoes in half; remove the pulp and mash it; and add enough hot milk to make it the consistency of mashed potatoes, and season it with salt. Fill the cases with this mixture; dot the top with butter; brush them with milk and bake the stuffed potatoes for 8 or 10 minutes in a hot oven or long enough to brown them on top. Potatoes may be stuffed in the morning and heated for the noon or evening meal.

Variations—To the mashed potatoes, before the cases are filled, may be added any one or a combination of the following:

Beaten white of egg (1 egg to 3 medium-sized potatoes).
Grated cheese (½ cup to 3 medium-sized potatoes).
Chopped meat (½ cup to 3 medium-sized potatoes).
Chopped parsley (1 tablespoon to 3 medium-sized potatoes).

SALSIFY OR OYSTER PLANT
Creamed Salsify or Oyster Plant

Boil salsify until tender, drain, and combine it with medium white sauce. Serve with tiny meat balls or little sausages.

Scalloped Salsify or Oyster Plant

Boil the salsify until tender. Cut it in slices one-half inch thick. Put a layer of buttered crumbs in the bottom of a buttered baking dish, cover with a layer of the slices of salsify, and add salt and pepper. Continue with alternate layers of the crumbs and salsify until the dish is full, covering the top with crumbs. Add enough hot milk to moisten. Bake in a moderate oven until the crumbs are well browned.

SPINACH
Spinach and Bacon

| 2 pounds spinach | Pepper |
| Salt | 6 slices bacon |

Prepare and cook spinach (steam in small amount of water or in waterless cooker). When tender, chop, season and add the bacon which has been cut in small pieces and cooked until crisp. A small amount of lemon juice may be added if desired.

Variations—The bacon may be omitted and ¼ cup of butter added just before serving. For creamed spinach add ¼ cup cream and 1 tablespoon of butter to the drained, chopped spinach and place the mixture on thin slices of crisp toast. Garnish the top with grated, hard-cooked egg or sliced egg.

TENDERGREEN
JAPANESE MUSTARD SPINACH

COMBINATION VEGETABLE RECIPES
With Eggs

16 eggs	1 pound green beans
1 pound diced carrots	2 pounds green peas
1 pound diced potatoes	1 pound baby limas
Mayonnaise, egg, oil, and lemon juice	

Boil the vegetables, tied in cheesecloth, in boiling salted water. Cook the eggs at simmering temperature until they are hard; shell, cut off the pointed end, remove the yolk and fill with mayonnaise. Run the yolk through a ricer and garnish the edge of a plate with this. Then put the eggs, filled with mayonnaise, inside of this. Fill the center of the dish with vegetables well marinated with the mayonnaise in the center, keeping each variety separate.—(French Selected.)

With Rabbit

1 rabbit (2 wild rabbits or large chicken)	¾ cup vinegar—flour
½ pound mushrooms	2 shallots or green onions
4 small onions	1 pound tomatoes, bouquet garnish
3 tablespoons butter	¾ cup bouillon
4 tablespoons oil	

Cut the rabbit into pieces, brown with oil, remove the rabbit and brown the onions and mushrooms and shallot; sprinkle with flour, add bouillon and vinegar, salt, pepper and rabbit, cover and cook slowly until tender.

One-quarter of an hour before serving add a sauce made from the tomatoes, bouquet and butter.

B.   General Recipes—Fruits
AVOCADO (SEE SALADS)
Toast

Mash the avocado, season with salt and lemon or lime juice and spread on hot toast and call it "Avocadoed Toast."

Soup

Butter the soup with avocado. Dice the avocado and add to the soup just before serving.

NOTE—Mayonnaise, cheese, nuts, butter are not needed when avocado is used. Use your own taste about other combinations. The avocado always needs salt and lime or lemon juice. It is a concentrated food, very rich in oil, nearly 18 per cent, and needs bread or other bulky food.

CITRUS FRUITS
Cooked Products

The fruits in many sections require additional pectin to produce jelly. Fortunately Florida has an abundant supply of pectin in citrus fruits.

It may be prepared for convenience as follows:

One-fourth pound white part of orange peel, ½ pint water, 2 tablespoons lemon juice.

Cut or grate the yellow from orange peel. Pass white peel through a food chopper. Weigh, add lemon juice, mix, allow to stand 1 hour. Add 1¼ pints water. Let stand 1 hour. Boil gently 10 minutes. Cover, let cool, place in flannel jelly bag. Press to remove juice. Drain juice through a clean bag.

The Pectin Test

To give the pectin test, pour 1 tablespoonful of jelly stock into clean cup. Pour into cup a teaspoon of grain alcohol (or denatured alcohol). Gently shake. Pour into a spoon. If the pectin shows a solid clot use one measure of sugar to one measure of juice. If it is not so solid use less sugar.

CITRUS FRUIT SPECIALS
Sour Orange Preserves

Grate the yellow from the peel. Cut the oranges in halves. Put four oranges into five quarts of water and boil 20 minutes. Change to fresh water and boil 15 minutes. Change and boil 10 minutes. Change again and boil 8 minutes. Drain and boil in sirup of one part sugar and two parts water until fruit is transparent. When sirup cooks to desired consistency, pour over fruit packed into sterilized jars and process 10 minutes. Seal.

Sour Orange Marmalade

1 pound peeled sour orange
2 pints water
⅓ of peel

1 cup sugar to 1 cup jelly stock or
less according to pectin test

Preparation of Peel—Wash fruit, remove peel, keeping ⅓ and slicing in thin slices. Leave some white on skins. Place in kettle. Add water 4 times weight of peel. Boil 10 minutes. Drain. Repeat 3 times, each time boiling 5 minutes. Continue until peel is very tender and all bitter taste removed.

Preparation of Jelly Stock—Weigh peeled fruit; cut into small pieces and, for each pound of orange, add 2 pints of water. Boil until thoroughly disintegrated. Drain in flannel jelly bag and press.

Making Marmalade—Pour juice into a kettle; add peel and bring to a boil. Make pectin test and add sugar as needed. Boil until the jellying point is reached.

Grapefruit Marmalade

1 pound peeled fruit
1 pound sugar (based on pectin test)

2 pints water
One-third of peel

This marmalade follows same directions as for sour oranges.

Combination Marmalade—Orange, Grapefruit, Lemon

2 oranges (pulp and peel)
1 lemon (pulp)

1 grapefruit (pulp)

Wash fruit. Grate yellow from oranges. Use white peel. Peel grapefruit and lemon and discard peel. Run fruit and orange peel through a chopper. Add 3 times the bulk of water. Boil 15 minutes and let stand over night. Boil 10 minutes and let stand again. When cold, measure pint for pint of sugar. Cook rapidly to jelly stage, 222° F. One cup grated pineapple, **previously boiled,** may be added.

Orange and Carrot Marmalade

3 cups carrots
½ teaspoon salt
4 cups sugar

2 oranges
3 lemons
1 cup water

Wash and scrape carrots and run through a food chopper. Boil until tender. Drain. Wash and peel oranges; chop one-half; strip the other. Boil strips until tender. Pour sugar over hot ground carrots. Let melt. Add water, lemon juice, orange pulp (cut in small pieces) and orange peel. Cook until sirup is thick and fruit is clear. Three slices of canned pineapple may be used instead of orange.

Florida Conserve

2 cups grapefruit pulp
2 cups orange pulp
¾ cup pecan meats

½ cup grated pineapple
2 cups sugar
Peel from 1 orange (chopped)

Preparation—To chopped peel add 1 cup water and boil 10 minutes. Cover. Let cool. (If fresh pineapple is used be sure to boil as it contains an enzyme that prevents the action of pectin unless the pineapple has reached boiling point.) Mix fruit pulp and orange peel; boil 20 minutes; add sugar. When dissolved, add pineapple. Cook to the jelly test. Add nuts. Pour into sterilized glasses and seal.

Kumquat Preserves

1 pound kumquats   ¾ pound sugar   3 cups water

Wash kumquats with soap and water. Sprinkle with soda (a tablespoon soda to 1 quart kumquats) and pour on boiling water and let stand 10 minutes. Pour off water. Rinse in 3 waters. Slit kumquats ¼ inch in side cutting seed cells. Place in kettle with water to cover. Boil 15 minutes. Repeat boiling process until fruit is tender. Drop kumquats into boiling sugar solution made by adding ¾ pound sugar to 3 cups water. Boil to 222°. Pack in jars. Strain sirup over fruit. Seal while hot. The fruit may be allowed to "plump" in the vessel covered for 25 minutes.

Kumquat Marmalade

Cook kumquat skins in water (changing 2 or 3 times if necessary) until tender.

Drain. Chop in meat chopper. Combine juice and peel, adding ¾ cup of sugar for each cup of fruit. Boil to jellying point.

Sunshine Marmalade

Remove the membranous skin or rag from the orange peel. Put through a food chopper. Add twice its weight in water and 2 tablespoons lemon juice for each cup of water. Let stand one hour and add same amount of water as first taken. Boil 3 minutes, cover, allow to cool. Press through a jelly bag. Keep one-half ground peel to add later to boiling juice. Test for pectin and add as much sugar as the test shows is needed. Use 1 cup juice to one cup sugar if there is solid clot. Bring to a boil. Add ½ of the ground peel and cook to 222° F.

FIGS

Fresh figs are best when first picked.

Breakfast Food

Serve ripe, peeled or unpeeled figs, with or without cream. No sugar is needed.

Preserving Figs

Select firm, sound, mature but not wholly ripe figs.

Fig Preserves

1 pound figs	1 pound sugar	4 cups water

Sort over and weigh. Wash dust from figs by placing in wire basket, or colander, and dipping in and out of boiling water. Add sugar in proportion of 1 pound to 1 pound of figs. Four cups of water. Cook, without stirring, to 224 degrees. Allow to stand, covered, over night, to "plump." Pack figs in sterilized jars. Fill to overflowing with sirup heated to boiling point. Partially seal and simmer 15 minutes for pints.

Lemon sliced through the peel may be added just before processing. Spices or ginger may be added but the real flavor of the fig is pleasing.

Sweet Spiced Figs

5 pints figs	1 stick cinnamon
1 pint water	1 teaspoon spice
1 cup vinegar	1 teaspoon mace
1 pint sugar	

Wash and dip figs as for preserving. Place in boiling water for a few minutes and add sugar, vinegar and spices. Cook to 222° or 224°, or until the figs are clear. Let stand over night. Pack and process 30 minutes at simmering temperature or 15 minutes at boiling point.

Fig Conserve

To 1 quart of broken figs and the juice and pulp of 2 lemons add 2 cups sugar and cook until right consistency for conserve. Add 2/3 cup pecan meats. Remove from heat. Pack and process 15 minutes at simmering.

NOTE—Grated lemon rind adds to the flavor.

Fig Spread

This is made from the broken figs or over-ripe stock. Clip off stems, run through a coarse food grinder. Measure. Place in heavy aluminum kettle and cook until thickened. Add ½ measure of sugar to one measure of fig pulp and cook to 221° F. Pack in hot jars, seal and process by boiling 5 minutes.

GRAPES

Grape Butter

Select and pulp ripe grapes. Heat the pulp with the juice and put them through a colander to remove the seeds. Add to the pulp and juice half a pound of sugar for every pound of fresh fruit. Cook the mixture until it is a jelly.

Canned Loquats, Halved

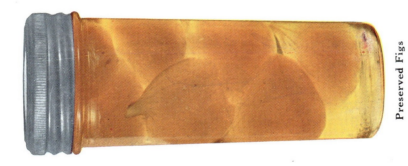

Preserved Figs

PLATE IX

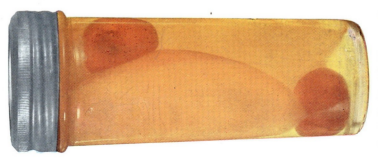

Grapefruit with Kumquats

Orange Marmalade

Calamondins

PLATE X

Kumquat Preserves

Mango Chutney

1 lb. peeled mangoes, cut in small
    pieces
1 pt. vinegar or ½ pt. grapefruit
    juice and ½ pt. vinegar
½ lb. currants
½ lb. raisins or 1 lb. raisins (if cur-
    rants are omitted)
¼ lb. blanched almonds
¾ lb. brown sugar

3 oz. green ginger sliced (may sub-
    stitute root ginger broken and
    put in spice bag)
1 tablespoon salt
½ tablespoon white mustard seed
½ cup chopped onions
½ cup chopped sweet peppers
1 oz. chillies or hot peppers

To the vinegar add sugar and bring to a boil. Add the spices, chopped vegetables, mangoes, nuts, raisins and salt, bring to a boil and boil for 30 minutes. Pack while at boiling point in sterilized jars and seal.

Mangoes just beginning to color are best selected.

Canned Mangoes

Select before the fruit shows color, or at initial stage. Peel, slice in convenient pieces, immerse in medium sirup for 1 to 2 minutes. Pack in jars, boil sirup to 218° F. and strain over fruit. Process 16 to 20 minutes at boiling. (Medium sirup, 1 cup sugar to 1 cup water.)

Mango Ice Cream

Use plain ice cream custard, made by any favorite recipe, as a basis. To each quart, add one pint of ripe mango pulp and freeze.

Mango Sundae

Have the fruit well iced. Cut in halves and remove the seed. Fill the cavity with ice cream (plain vanilla is best), and serve at once.

Cooked Mangoes

Mango for pies, sauces and butters. Select mature but unripe mangoes and use in recipes for green apples. Sweeten according to taste.

PAPAYA

Papaya Sauce

Select the melon at a mature but unripe stage. Boil or stem and add a little lime juice. This makes a delicious French sauce. The unripe fruit may be used like any other melon in pickles or preserves. It combines nicely with other fruits for marmalades and jellies. It is very good for sherbets. As a breakfast food it needs no additions. As a dessert it is perfect.

Baked Papaya

Cut mature but unripe papaya in halves lengthwise. Add a little sugar and orange, lime or lemon juice; or a little cinnamon in place of the juice. Bake 20 minutes and serve immediately on taking from the oven.

Papaya Pickle

1 cup sugar
2 cups water

1 cup vinegar
3 cups papaya

Make sirup of sugar and vinegar and water. Add a few whole cloves and pepper-corns and half-ripe papaya cut into small pieces. Boil until tender. Ginger or lemon may be added.

Papaya Whip

To 1½ cups papaya pulp add juice of 1 lemon, ½ cup sugar, and beat into 2 stiffly whipped whites of eggs. Cook. Serve with whipped cream.

Papaya Butter

Take ripe papaya—peel, seed, cut in small pieces—slightly cover with water, cook until tender. Put through fruit press. To each cup of pulp add ½ cup of sugar, juice from one lemon, cook to 222° F. Pack in jars. Process 15 minutes.

Lime in Papaya Butter

To every 2 cups ripe mashed papaya add ¼ cup lime juice and 1 cup sugar.

PEACHES
Canned

Peaches are canned in a thin sirup in halves or whole for desserts and salads, and in pieces for pies and other cooked dishes.

Sweet Pickled Peaches

6 pounds peaches	4 ounces stick cinnamon
6 cups water	2 pounds whole cloves
2 cups vinegar	Ginger root
6 cups sugar	

Select firm clingstone peaches. Peel and drop into sirup of sugar, water and vinegar, boiled together. Cook to 221°. Pack. Cover with boiling hot sirup and process 20 minutes at simmering.

Peach Preserves

3 lbs. peeled, sliced, clingstone peaches	2 pounds sugar
6 cups water	3 peach kernels

Bring sugar and water to a boil, add peaches. Cook to 222°. Let "plump" over night. Pack in sterilized containers, seal and process, or pack while hot.

Peach Butter

Wash 4 quarts ripe peaches thoroughly. Cut in pieces and put through dilver. To each pint of pulp add 1 cup of sugar. Cook until of the desired consistency. Pour into sterilized jars and process 15 minutes.

Peach Chutney

1 dozen ripe peaches	2 quarts vinegar
1 red pepper	1 cup sugar
1 hot pepper	½ tablespoon ginger
1 green pepper	½ tablespoon cinnamon
½ pound raisins	½ tablespoon spice
3 onions (mild)	½ tablespoon celery seed
½ cup acid fruit juice	Salt

Combine ingredients and cook until the mixture is quite thick and clear. Pack hot, seal and process 15 minutes at simmering.

Peach—Pineapple—Lemon

2 dozen peaches chopped	6 cups sugar
1 pineapple or 1 pint can	2 lemons (juice and rind)

Cook peaches thick before adding other ingredients. Cook entire mixture until quite thick.

Two cups of pecan meats may be added while mixture is boiling hot. Pack, seal, process 5 minutes. A conserve may be made by using ripe peaches and shredded pineapple. The addition of seedless raisins or of shredded fig preserves adds to the interest and lessens the amount of sugar needed. Lemon will give an additional flavor.

PEARS
Canned

Peel from stem to blossom, placing immediately in weak salt solution (2 tablespoons to a gallon). Cut into halves and remove cores. Cook 5 to 10 minutes in syrup of one part sugar to two parts water. Pack into quart jars and process 20 minutes, depending upon tenderness of fruit. If lemon or ginger flavor is desired, add while cooking.

Preserved Pears

1 pound pears   ¾ pound sugar   3 cups water

Cut pears in halves and core; place in syrup of sugar and water and cook to 224° F. Allow to stand until plump. Pack and process 20 minutes. Whole cloves, slices of lemon or ginger may be added.

Pickled Pears

3 pounds firm pears   1 tablespoon ginger
4 cups sugar   A few whole cloves
3 cups vinegar   1 tablespoon spices (whole)
5 cups water   A stick of cinnamon
½ lemon

Peel pears lengthwise and leave whole. Make syrup of vinegar, water and sugar; tie the spice in small pieces of cheesecloth, and add to the syrup. When this mixture begins to simmer, add the pears and lemon rind and bring to 222°. Cool and let stand. The next morning, drain off the syrup and bring the syrup to boiling point. Pack fruit in jars, garnish with cinnamon, cover with the syrup, seal and process quarts for 15 minutes at 180° Fahrenheit (simmering).

Baked Pears

Core firm, medium-sized pears. Place in covered baking dish, sprinkle with brown sugar. Add stick of cinnamon. Allow enough water to cover bottom of pan. When tender, remove pears to glass dish, cook down syrup and pour over pears. Serve hot or cold.

PINEAPPLE (SEE SALADS)

Pineapple, because of its enzymes, combines nicely with meats or omelets. Broiled ham or small sausages are often served on slices of pineapple or with a sauce made of shredded pineapple.

Pineapple Omelet

7 eggs   ¾ cup grated cheese
1 teaspoon salt   1½ tablespoons fat
3 tablespoons milk or cream   1½ cups crushed canned pineapple

Separate eggs; beat yolks for one minute; then add salt, milk or cream, and cheese and continue beating until well mixed. Melt fat in frying or omelet pan, turning pan so melted fat goes well up on the sides. Beat whites of eggs until stiff and fold in the yolk and cheese mixture. Pour into the pan and cook over low heat until nicely browned on the underside. Then place in a slow oven for about three minutes to dry off top. Meanwhile put the undrained pineapple into a sauce pan and boil until thick, about ten minutes. When omelet is done, make a cut about one and one-half inches long on either end of the fold line; then pour pineapple on one-half of the omelet, fold and slide onto platter.

Pineapple Luncheon Sandwiches

1 cup finely diced cooked ham   1 tablespoon prepared mustard
1 cup crushed canned pineapple, drained 2 tablespoons pineapple juice
2 tablespoons milk or water   1 beaten egg

Mix first four ingredients together well and spread between slices of buttered bread. Dip each side of the prepared sandwiches in the beaten egg which has been combined with milk; sauté until golden brown on both sides. Serve at once.

Pineapple and Rhubarb Marmalade

NOTE—If fresh pineapple is used in any of these recipes for marmalades, remember to bring to a boil before combining with other fruits.

3 lbs. pink rhubarb   4 cups sugar
3 cups pineapple pieces   Juice and grated rind 1 lemon

Rhubarb need not be peeled if young and tender. Wash, and cut into inch pieces. Drain pineapple. Combine rhubarb, pineapple, sugar and lemon. Cook slowly until thick and clear. Fill jelly glasses and cover with paraffin.

Pineapple Sauce

2 cups crushed canned pineapple, undrained
½ cup pineapple juice or water
⅓ cup of sugar
Juice and rind of 1 lemon
1 tablespoon cornstarch

Heat pineapple, pineapple juice, grated lemon rind and lemon juice until boiling. Combine cornstarch and sugar and add to pineapple sauce, stirring constantly. Cook until thickened, and serve hot.

Pineapple-Strawberry Conserve

1 quart strawberries
1 pint spiced grapes
2 cups pineapple pieces
1 orange
Sugar

Wash and hull berries. Drain grapes. Drain pineapple from juice. Slice orange very thin or put through food chopper. Combine fruit, weigh, and add an equal weight of sugar. Cook slowly until mixture thickens when a little is tested on a cold plate. Pour into hot glasses and cover with melted paraffin. This is a delicious preserve to serve with cream cheese and crackers.

Pineapple With Orange Sections

1 slice fresh pineapple
Powdered sugar
Orange sections

Chill pineapple and orange. Peel orange with a sharp knife, cutting through the white inner skin. Remove sections, keeping in as large pieces as possible. When ready to serve, lay slices of pineapple on individual plates, put a small mound of powdered sugar in the center and arrange orange sections around pineapple slices, making a complete circle. Serve cold.

Pineapple Dessert

4 cups shredded pineapple
12 marshmallows
Pecans
Strawberry jam
Whipped cream

In each dessert glass put a layer of shredded pineapple, then 2 marshmallows, cut in pieces with scissors dipped in cold water. Next a layer of jam, another layer of shredded pineapple. Top with whipped cream, sweetened and flavored. Sprinkle with chopped nuts or cocoanut.

STRAWBERRY PRESERVES

1 pound berries   ¾ pound sugar

Select large, firm fruit. Wash, cap, getting the pithy center if possible. Place berries in aluminum or porcelain vessel. Add sugar. Handle vessel over flame so that the juice reaches the sugar and dissolves to form a syrup or let stand over night. Place vessel over flame and bring to boil and boil 8 minutes. Cover and set aside until fruit is plump and cool. Cook to desired consistency. Pack and seal.

STRAWBERRY JAM

Wash, cap and crush ripe strawberries. To each pound of fruit add ¾ pound of sugar. Stir constantly and cook to 222° F. or until desired consistency.

LOQUAT PRESERVES

1 pound fruit   ¾ pint water   ¾ pound sugar

Wash, scald, peel and seed fruit. Make a syrup of sugar and water. Add fruit and cook to 226° F. Put in hot sterilized containers. Seal and process 15 minutes.

LOQUAT JAM

1 pound fruit   ¾ pound sugar   ½ pint water

Prepare as for preserves. Put through food chopper. Mix sugar and water. Add fruit and cook to about 225½° F. or jellying point. Seal.

ROSELLE SAUCE

Use equal measures of fruit and water and cook until tender, about 10 minutes. Sweeten to taste. Allow to come again to boiling point. It is not necessary to strain the product.

FRUIT JUICES—CANNED

Grapefruit Hearts

Grapefruit juice, in canning includes the "hearts." Grapefruit hearts are now known throughout the country. Prepare as for salads, removing the hearts whole. Pack tightly into pint jars in which has been placed 2 tablespoons sugar. Process 35 minutes, 180°.

Grapefruit Juice

Extract juice in such way as to exclude oil of the peel or the bitterness of the rag. Bring juice to 165° or 170° in open vessel. Fill into bottles boiling hot. Cap quickly. Process in water at 180° F. for 30 minutes.

Orange Juice

Sweet orange juice keeps its flavor better in canning when combined with sour citrus juice in proportion of 4 to 1. Lime, lemon, calamondin, Seville or sour orange may be used. Use sugar in proportion of 2 cups sugar to one gallon juice mixture. Bottle and process at 165° F. for 30 minutes.

OTHER FRUIT JUICES

Ripe grapes, plums, berries produce valuable fruit juices. Bring fruit to simmering temperature. Remove juice, strain through a heavy cloth. Sweeten slightly, about 1 cup sugar to a gallon of juice. Strain again if a clear juice is desired. Seal hot and process at about 180° F. Fruit jars may be used for keeping juices for home use. If bottles are used, cork tightly, process and seal with wax afterwards, or use a bottle capper.

Fruits Containing Pectin for Jelly—Citrus fruits, particularly ripened grapes, blackberries, dewberries, huckleberries, quinces, guavas, crabapple, May haws, plums, pomegranate, roselle.

Fruits Lacking in Pectin—Strawberries, peaches, pineapple, rhubarb.

Fruits Lacking Acid for Jelly—Pears, quince, sugar apple, sapodilla, sweet guava.

Tropical Fruits for Jelly—Tamarind (red), satin fruit (red), pitanga (red), mulberry (dark), guava, carambola, Persian lime, pomegranate, Cattley guava, jaboticaba, umkokolo, ketembilla (English gooseberry).

C. A Few Florida Fruit Desserts

Numerous of the sweet, sub-acid and acid fruits lend themselves easily to desserts. The sapote, the sapodilla, sugar apple, the mango, papaya, in the natural form, are desserts. The sour-sop, the lime, the pomegranate, the tamarind, the passion flower lend a delightful flavor to sherbets. The juicy fruits, berries, citrus, plums and grapes are adaptable in hundreds of methods. The melons, guavas, peaches, pears, figs, greatly increase the list. The rich Florida coloring in fruits gives wonderful possibilities in attractiveness.

Since many vegetables must be cooked, fruits remain the sure means of getting Nature's fresh natural food with the vitamins, mineral, organic acids and laxative properties. Therefore, it is important that fruits be used fresh. They are also used to flavor and make attractive other less interesting foods.

The best known Florida dessert—that is, the dessert most nearly a Florida dessert—is ambrosia.

AMBROSIA

6 oranges   ½ cup sugar   3 cups fresh grated cocoanut

Peel and slice pulp of oranges. Grate cocoanut. Place a layer of orange pulp in a large bowl. Sprinkle a little sugar and add a layer of cocoanut, then another layer of orange, a sprinkle of sugar, and over all pour cocoanut juice and free orange juice. Add a final covering of grated cocoanut. Leave in refrigerator until next day and serve.

ORANGE FRAPPE

2 cups sugar   2 cups orange juice
3 cups water   ½ cup lemon juice

Boil sugar and water 10 minutes. Cool, add fruit juices. Freeze to a mush.

LEMON SHERBET
(Makes about 1¾ quarts)

3 cups sugar   ¾ cup lemon juice
1 quart water   2 egg whites

Boil sugar and water together for 5 minutes to make syrup. Add lemon juice, cool and freeze to a mush. Add stiffly beaten egg whites and finish freezing.

FRUIT SHERBET

¼ cup orange juice   1 cup any one of the following fruits:
½ cup lemon juice   Crushed strawberries, crushed
2½ cups sugar   peaches, mashed bananas, man-
1 quart milk   goes, guavas, papayas.
                           Add more sugar, if needed

Mix and freeze. If mixture curdles it will freeze smooth again.

ORANGE ICE CREAM

3 cups orange juice   1 cup thick cream
1 cup sugar   2 cups thin cream or milk

Mix orange juice and sugar thoroughly. Add cream or cream and milk and freeze. Or add just thin cream or milk, freeze to a mush; add whipped cream and continue freezing.

ORANGE CREAM CUSTARD
(Serves 6)

2 eggs   2 cups milk
¼ cup sugar   ½ teaspoon vanilla
2 teaspoons flour   5 tablespoons sugar
⅛ teaspoon salt   4 oranges

Beat egg yolks, add ¼ cup sugar, flour and salt and mix thoroughly. Add milk and cook in double boiler until thick enough to coat spoon. Cool, add vanilla and turn into serving dish containing peeled and sliced oranges. Beat egg whites with 5 tablespoons sugar. Heap on top of custard and serve.

ORANGE BAVARIAN CREAM

1 tablespoon granulated gelatine   ½ cup sugar
¼ cup cold water   Sprinkling salt
1 cup orange juice and pulp   1 cup cream
1 tablespoon lime juice

Soak gelatine in cold water for 5 minutes and dissolve by standing cup containing mixture in hot water. Add to orange juice and pulp. Add lime juice, sugar and salt. When it begins to jelly, fold in whipped cream; turn into cold mold to become firm.

ORANGE BAVARIAN CREAM PIE

Make orange Bavarian cream as given in recipe, pouring into baked pastry shell. Chill till firm. Top with additional whipped cream if desired.

LEMON FLUFF PIE

3 eggs
⅓ cup lemon juice
Grated rind 1 lemon

3 tablespoons hot water
¼ teaspoon salt
1 cup sugar

Beat yolks of eggs very light. Add lemon juice and grated rind, hot water, salt and ½ cup sugar. Cook in double boiler until thick. Add ½ cup sugar to stiffly beaten egg whites and fold into cooked mixture. Fill baked pie shell and brown in moderate oven.

FRUIT CAKE

This recipe is recommended as a simple and inexpensive cake, but a very good one.

1 lb. seeded raisins
1 lb. currants
1 lb. sliced citron
1 lb. sliced orange peel (crystallized)
1 cup chopped crystallized fig
1 lb. pecan meats
4 cups (1 lb.) flour
4 cups (1½ lbs.) brown sugar
1 dozen eggs

2 teaspoons salt
2 teaspoons baking powder
2 teaspoons cinnamon
2 teaspoons mace
1 teaspoon nutmeg
1 teaspoon allspice
½ teaspoon cloves
1 lb. butter or other fat
½ cup cider or other fruit juice

Prepare the fruit and nuts according to the general directions. Mix the flour, salt, baking powder and spices; sift about half of this mixture over the fruit and mix with the finger tips.

Cream the fat; add the sugar gradually, then the beaten eggs. Stir in flour alternately with the fruit juice. Add the floured fruit and nuts. Bake according to general directions.

Weight of baked cake: About 12 pounds.

D. Crystallized Fruits

Directions for crystallizing fruit when it is desired to keep the fruit for a long period of time:

Preparation of Fruit—All citrus fruits should be of a bright color, without blemish and with thick peel. Grapefruit, lemon, oranges and limes must be grated sufficiently to break the oil cells. The bitter in the peel is removed by putting the peel on in cold water, letting it come to a boil, and then by draining off, changing the water and starting over each time with cold water. The number of changes depends on the individual taste. The peel should be tender before it goes into the sirup.

Kumquats—Wash, treat with a hot soda bath (one tablespoon of soda to one pound of fruit. Cover with boiling water. Let stand until cool. Wash in clear water. Make a small slit in the sides of the kumquats, cutting through the seed cells. Cover with water, then cook until tender before putting into the sirup.

Pineapples—Peel, cut in one-half inch slices, core and boil until tender.

Fig, Watermelon Rind and Other Fruits—Treat as you would in preparing for preserves.

Quick Method for Immediate Consumption

Make a thin sirup, 2 parts water, 1 part sugar, (sufficient to cover the fruit after the sirup is cooked down). Put fruit on and cook until clear. Cook down to 220° F. first day. Let stand in this sirup for at least 24 hours. Then cook to 226° F. Let stand in this sirup until next day. Then cook to 228° F.; take out, shape and put in sun to dry. When partially dry roll in granulated sugar and put back in sun or in a good place to dry.

Continued Method for Marketing

To make a marketable product when the fruit is cooked to 226° F. put in jars and process for 15 minutes. Seal and keep this preserve until you are ready to crystallize it.

To finsh product make a 222° sirup and put the drained fruit into the sirup and cook to 226° F. Drain shape and place in sun to dry. When partially dry roll in granulated sugar. This method will take longer to dry, but the product will keep much longer.

Coloring and flavoring may be used, but it cheapens the product and causes the fruit to lose its identity if overdone. Eight drops of any standard vegetable coloring to the pound of sugar put into the sirup is sufficient to give a delicate shade to the finished product. If flavorings are used, add to the product the last five minutes of cooking.

For pineapple, whole limes, etc., preserve in 235° F. sirup and finish in a 250° F. sirup. As soon as the desired temperature is reached, remove from fire and stir until moderately cool. Remove the fruit, which will be coated in fondant, and dry.

GRAPEFRUIT PEEL STRIPS

1 lb. grapefruit peel
1 lb. sugar

6 tablespoons liquid $\begin{cases} 3 \text{ fruit juice} \\ 3 \text{ water} \end{cases}$

Preparation of Peel—Select bright fruit with a thick peel. Wash carefully. Grate lightly on an ordinary grater to break the oil cells. Cut this peel into strips that are ¼ to ½ inch in width; or into small shapes. To remove the bitter, place in pan of cold water and let come to a boil. Change water as many times as necessary, starting each time in cold water. When fruit is tender, drain and weigh.

For each pound of peel add 1 pound of sugar and 6 tablespoons of liquid; cook until the sirup is absorbed. Remove from the fire and roll in granulated sugar and lay on platter to dry.

Finishing Point—If cooking is continued for too long a period of time and evaporation carried too far, the product will be hard and unattractive. The point at which the product is finished may be determined by rolling a piece of the fruit, when it has become transparent, in granulated sugar. If, after a few minutes, the fruit stiffens enough to retain its shape, it is sufficiently cooked. A strip of the peel is preferred to the small shapes in making this test.

NOTE—If it is desired to give a variety in appearance to the finished product, the peel may be cut into small attractive shapes, before being boiled. Vegetable coloring may be added to the sirup in which the peel is crystallized. Mint ginger or other flavoring may be blended with the grapefruit flavor by adding to the sirup.

Suggestions For Using Florida Fruits

Written and Compiled by
Office of Home Demonstration Work, Florida Agricultural Extension Service
May, 1938

Advances made in the science of nutrition in the last twenty years have probably interested more people than have similar advances in other fields of human endeavor. Certainly there is today more intelligent interest taken in foods than was dreamed of even ten years ago. Today the American public is consuming many more fruit and vegetable products than formerly. This indicates that the average person looks upon fruits and vegetables as essential to health and well being.*

THE COLORFUL PITANGA OR SURINAM-CHERRY

While the surinam-cherry in Florida is frequently grown for decorative purposes, the fruit may be cooked and used as a sauce or may be made into jam, preserves or jelly. Because of the tart flavor, the sauce resembles that made from cranberries and the jelly or tart sherbet made from the cherry juice is best served with meat or fowl. Combined with the apple and other fruits, the cherries may be used for pies or puddings. The juice, prepared as for jelly making, may be used as a foundation for an iced drink. The juice of the firm-ripe cherries gives a good test for pectin. The fruit seems to develop a bitter taste on standing so they should be used just as soon after picking as possible. It is very important also that the fruit be used fully matured for best and most agreeable flavor.

Surinam-Cherry Jam

3¾ cups seeded surinam-cherries   2 cups water
3¾ cups sugar

Combine the sugar and water, bring to the boiling point, and add cherries. Boil for 20 to 25 minutes or until the juice thickens slightly, but not until it gives the jelly test (sheets off the spoon in large drops.)

Pour into hot, sterile jars and seal immediately.

Surinam-Cherry Jelly

Surinam-cherries   Sugar
Enough water to barely cover the fruit

Wash cherries and crush lightly. Add water to the fruit and simmer gently for 20 minutes or until the cherries are soft. Allow to stand 20 minutes. Strain the juice through a flannel jelly bag or two thicknesses of cheese cloth.

Measure the juice and place it in a shallow kettle with a capacity at least 4 times the volume of juice. Add an equal quantity of sugar and remove the scum as the mixture starts to boil. Boil rapidly until the juice gives the jelly test (sheets off the spoon in large drops), or until the temperature reaches 105° C., or 221° F. Pour the jelly into hot, sterile glasses and seal immediately.

It is important that the cherries be freshly gathered and not over-ripe.

Surinam-Cherry Pie

1¼ cups seeded Surinam-cherries   1⅛ cups sugar
½ cup seedless raisins   2 tablespoons flour
¾ cup diced apple   2 tablespoons butter

Line a pie tin with pastry. Mix the fruit and pour into the pie shell. Sprinkle with flour and sugar and dot with small pieces of butter. Moisten the edge of the pie crust and cover with a second crust. Place in a hot oven (450° F.) for 10 minutes, then reduce the temperature to 350° F. and bake for 30 to 40 minutes or until the fruit is soft and the crust lightly browned.

---

*For recipes on guavas, papayas, mangoes, and avocados see the bulletins on these fruits.

THE LUSCIOUSNESS OF PERSIMMONS

The season for the luscious red-gold Japanese persimmons, the Fuyugaki, non-astringent, and the Tane-Nashi, Triumph, Tamopan, Tsuru and others of the astringent class comes in the fall of the year. The Fuyugaki may be used as soon as it is fully colored and mature, but still firm to the touch. It may be peeled, diced and used in a fruit salad just as an apple is used and will be found tender, sweet, crisp and delicately flavored. The astringent varieties should never be picked until they are colored a deep gold and should be kept until soft, transparent and of the consistency of jelly. When fully ripe they will be found rich-flavored and sweet. By a thoughtful combination of the persimmon with other fruits and vegetables, results may be obtained that are as delightful to the sense of taste as to the sight.

Florida people and others should more fully appreciate the lusciousness of this easy to grow food-fruit and enjoy them as a liberal part of the fruit requirements. They are fine served with sugar and cream and in combination salads. When served at the table without previous preparation, the usual way of proceeding is to place the fruit stem end down on a dessert plate, cut away a bit of the skin from the blossom end or top, and eat the fruit with a spoon, removing it from the skin. Crackers and cream or Camembert cheese make a good accompaniment served thus.

Persimmon and Grapefruit Salad

Select soft, transparent persimmons. Peel by beginning at the blossom end and work toward the stem in order that the fruit may hold its shape. Cut into sections the size of grapefruit sections. If not using canned grapefruit sections, prepare the fresh fruit by cutting away all skin and membrane from each section of "heart" using a **very sharp knife.**

On the salad plate arrange a bed of shredded lettuce, endive or cabbage and on it alternate the persimmon and grapefruit sections around a central point to make the salad to resemble a flower, using a spoonful of mayonnaise in the center to complete the flower idea. Serve with either a peppy French dressing or a fruit mayonnaise. This is a most delicious salad and suits admirably with a hearty dinner.

Molded Persimmon and Pineapple Salad

Peel three very ripe persimmons. Incorporate this pulp to contents of one package of pineapple or lemon flavored gelatine dissolved in 1½ cupfuls of hot water and cooled. Boiling hot pineapple juice may be used with lemon gelatine instead of the boiling water, and crushed pineapple may be added to the persimmon pulp. Chill, turn out, and serve garnished with pineapple or grapefruit segments and mayonnaise or cooked salad dressing mixed with whipped cream. This is a beautiful, luscious, colorful salad.

Golden Glow Salad

This delicious persimmon salad calls for a package of orange or lime flavored prepared gelatine. Dissolve in one cup of boiling water as directed on the box. Stir the mixture until gelatine is dissolved, then add ¾ cup of grapefruit juice. When beginning to congeal, stir in 1 cup of ripe persimmons that have been peeled and placed in the refrigerator to become firm. Allow molds time to become thoroughly firm or the effect is lost. When ready to serve, turn out on crisp lettuce leaves or shredded cabbage, fill with cottage cheese and top with mayonnaise. Pass French dressing also.

Persimmon Ice

This is attractive, cooling and refreshing on warm autumn days. It also may be made in either a crank freezer or a refrigerator.

2 tablespoonfuls of gelatine	1½ pints of grapefruit juice
1¾ cupfuls sugar	1½ pints of persimmon pulp (riced
1 pint boiling water	or run through the colander)

Soak the gelatine 5 minutes in ½ cupful of cold water, adding the boiling water and sugar, stir well and let cool, then add the grapefruit juice and freeze until like mush. Fold in the peeled and riced persimmons and continue freezing until firm. Pack and allow the ice to stand for several hours before serving. In making persimmon ice, special care should be used to select thoroughly ripe fruit.

Persimmon-a-la-mode

If the fruit is fine and large like the Tamopan, it may be kept on ice, then cut in halves and served with a scoop of vanilla ice cream—a dish fit for a King!

Persimmon Ice Cream No. 1

Beat together thoroughly 2 cups of persimmon pulp, 1 cup sugar and one cup of thick, sweet cream, and freeze in a rotary freezer. The fruit must be thoroughly ripe. Ripe persimmon pulp may be used by the local ice cream manufacturer like peach or guava pulp in ice cream.

Persimmon Fruit Ice Cream No. 2

1 pint coffee cream
½ pint orange juice

½ pint strained persimmon pulp

Sweeten to taste and freeze in usual way.

Persimmon Fruit Ice

Beat 2 cups of persimmon pulp, 1 cup of sugar and one-half cup of water to a creamy pulp and freeze in a rotary freezer.

Persimmon Cream Pie

3 very soft persimmons
2 eggs
2 cupfuls of rich milk or cream

½ cupful or more of sugar
⅛ teaspoon of salt

Wash the persimmons and put through a ricer or rub through a colander. Beat the eggs, add the sugar and salt and mix well. Add the cream or milk and the mashed persimmons. Pour into a partly baked pie crust, dot 4 teaspoonfuls of butter over the top, and finish baking in a moderate oven (375° F.) until the custard is set.

Persimmon Pudding No. 1

The following recipe is a favorite of the middle west where the small wild persimmons grow in profusion and which must be touched with frost before they are eaten. Made with the cultivated persimmon, we find the results much the same.

2 eggs
¾ cup sugar
1 pint persimmon pulp peeled and
    riced
1 pint sweet milk
¼ cup melted butter
¾ cup chopped black walnuts or
    pecans

½ teaspoon baking soda
2 cups flour
1 teaspoon baking powder
¼ teaspoon cinnamon and nutmeg
¼ teaspoon salt

Beat eggs, add sugar, persimmon pulp, milk and melted butter. Stir together dry ingredients, add the chopped nuts and add to the first mixture, beating only enough to blend well. Pour into a shallow greased pan and bake 40 minutes in a moderate oven (350° to 400° F.). The pudding may be served with whipped cream or a pudding sauce.

Persimmon Pudding No. 2

1 cup sugar
1 cup milk
1 cup flour
1½ teaspoons baking powder

1 cup persimmon pulp, strained
¼ teaspoon soda
2 tablespoons melted butter
1 teaspoon vanilla

Mix and steam one hour in half-pound baking powder cans.

ROSELLE OR FLORIDA CRANBERRY

The roselle carries the names of Florida cranberry, "lemon bush," "red sorrel" or "Jamaica sorrel." It is very sensitive to frost and can be grown only in tropical and sub-tropical climates. The edible portion is the large, fleshy red calyx. The blossom fades within one day and the calyxes are ready for picking about three weeks after the bloom appears. There are some latent buds on the stems and if the calyxes are picked as soon as they are full grown these buds develop. In this way the close of the roselle season in Florida may be extended from December well into February, provided, of course, there are no frosts.

The chemical analyses show roselle to be very similar in composition to the cranberry, the most important difference being that the cranberry contains benzoic acid and roselle does not. Roselle makes a jelly and a sauce very similar in color, texture and flavor to cranberries, hence the name.

Remove the seed pod before cooking. It is easily forced out by cutting off the stem end of the calyx where it is joined to the pod and pressing gently with the fingers, or by cutting both stem end and side of calyx and removing with the fingers. Don't over-cook roselle! Over-cooking just as over-maturity, robs roselle of its finest flavor and toughens it. Properly cooked it is bright red in color, deliciously tender and appetizing. Roselle furnishes a delightful fruit sauce to serve with all meats and poultry. It may also be used as the basis of many tempting salads and desserts.

Roselle Sauce

About ten minutes boiling or less gives a tender product. When roselle is to be served as a sauce, use equal measures of calyxes and of water. Cook until tender, sweeten to taste, and allow sauce to come again to the boiling point in order to be certain that all the sugar is dissolved. The sauce may be rubbed through a coarse sieve and the sugar added to the strained product. This gives a very excellent imitation of strained cranberry sauce.

A spicy sauce may be made by using less water when putting calyxes on to cook and substitute vinegar for the amount deducted, adding ground cinnamon, cloves and allspice to flavor.

Roselle Jelly

Roselle makes a beautiful jelly of a very tender texture. The jelling point seems to be easily lost by over-cooking and the jelly must, therefore, be removed promptly from the fire when the jelling point has been reached. Two measures of water for one of calyxes is the proportion used for making the extraction. After boiling ten minutes cover and allow the roselle to cool before straining. Use a low jelly glass, if the product is to be removed from the glass for serving.

Sauce may be made from the dried product found on the market, but this does not make a tender sauce after it has been kept for a long time.

Jellied Roselle Salad

1 quart roselle (with seed pods removed)	⅓ cup cold water
	Lettuce
2 cups boiling water	1 cup diced celery
2 cups sugar	⅓ cup chopped pecan meats
2 tablespoons granulated gelatine	Mayonnaise or boiled dressing

Cook together the roselle calyxes and water for twenty minutes. Rub through a sieve, stir in the sugar, and cook five minutes. Add gelatine which has been dissolved in the cold water for five minutes, and just before this begins to set, pour half of the mixture into a shallow glass or enamelware dish, which has been rinsed in cold water. Allow it to set, keeping the remainder warm to prevent it from becoming stiff. Over the first half, sprinkle the diced celery and nut meats. Pour the remaining half over this and allow it to set. Cut into slices and serve on the lettuce leaves with a garnish of salad dressing and a few extra nut meats.

Roselle Salad

On a chilled plate, arrange crisp lettuce leaves. In the center put a good big spoonful of stiff roselle sauce and sprinkle over with cream cheese which has been put through a sieve. Add chopped pecans as a top garnish and serve with French dressing made with lemon juice instead of vinegar.

Roselle Sponge

Stew one quart of roselle, with seed pods removed, in a pint of water until soft. Rub through a colander. Add 1 cup of sugar and return to stove, then add boiling hot to three tablespoons of gelatine which has been soaked in ½ cup cold water. Pour half the mixture in a wet jelly mold and set in cold water to stiffen. When the remainder is partly stiffened, whip it with Dover egg beater until it is a mass of fluff, and pour it lightly over the first. Set to cool, then place on ice. Serve with sweet orange sauce.

Orange Sauce

1¾ cups sugar
2 cups hot water
2 tablespoons lemon juice
2 tablespoons butter

4 tablespoons flour
½ teaspoon grated orange rind
1 cup orange juice

Mix sugar, orange rind and flour; add hot water slowly and bring to boiling point, stirring. Boil 8 minutes, add lemon and orange juice and butter. Serve.

Mock Cherry Pie

2½ cups roselle with seed pods removed
1 cup sugar
½ cup raisins

1½ cups boiling water
2 tablespoons flour

Mix raisins, roselle, and water and cook ten minutes. Then add flour to sugar and mix well. Combine with other ingredients and cook until thickened. Add 1 tablespoonful butter. Bake with two crusts in a hot oven, or fill a baked shell, cover with meringue and place in a cool oven for ten minutes or until slightly browned.

THE POPULAR COCOANUT

Fresh cocoanuts are available all the year around in extreme South Florida from the home yard, and they may be purchased in all the larger markets and at the majority of the roadside stands. At the large markets the cocoanut will be freshly grated for the waiting customer.

For all that cocoanuts are plentiful, fresh cocoanut pies, cakes, puddings, frozen desserts, candies and icings are not as generally and as frequently served as their universal popularity would seem to warrant. No doubt the labor and time required to prepare them is responsible for this situation.

Cocoanuts may be used in different stages of ripeness. The young nuts, called "spoon cocoanuts" which have a thin layer of very soft meat, may be chilled and served from the shell or may be used as individual containers for fruit cocktails.

Papaya-Cocoanut Pudding

1⅓ cups papaya pulp
3 cups shredded cocoanut
    (1 cocoanut yields about 1⅓
    cups cocoanut milk)

¾ cup sugar
6 tablespoons cornstarch
1 cup boiling water

Pour boiling water over shredded cocoanut and allow to remain 15 to 30 minutes. Strain through several thicknesses of cheesecloth, squeezing out as much liquid as possible.

Press the papaya pulp through a sieve and then measure it. Mix the cornstarch, sugar, and salt together, stir into the papaya and cook over a low flame, stirring constantly until it thickens. Add the cocoanut milk and cook 5 to 10 minutes until the mixture is thick enough to be served with a tablespoon and hold its shape when cool. It should not be stiff enough to mold. Pour mixture into a deep dish or pan and chill. Thick cocoanut milk may be served over the pudding if desired.

Favorite Cocoanut Cream Pie No. 1

2 cups milk
3 egg yolks
¾ cup sugar
1/16 teaspoon salt

3 tablespoons cornstarch
½ teaspoon vanilla
¼ cup whipping cream
¾ cup fresh grated cocoanut

Combine the sugar, corn starch and salt. Scald the milk and add the dry ingredients slowly to the hot milk, stirring until a smooth mixture is obtained. Cook over hot water, stirring frequently. Cool the mixture to lukewarm and stir in the egg yolks. Cook over hot water until the custard thickens. Cool, add vanilla, and pour into a baked pie shell. Chill and whip the cream. Just before serving spread the custard with the whipped cream and sprinkle with cocoanut.

Cocoanut Cream Pie No. 2

2/3 tablespoon gelatine
3 tablespoons water
1⅓ cups scalded milk
2 eggs

¼ cup sugar
1/16 teaspoon salt
½ teaspoon vanilla
¾ cup fresh grated cocoanut

Soak gelatine in the cold water. Add sugar and salt to egg yolks and slowly add the milk. Cook this mixture over hot water, stirring until the custard mixture thickens and coats the spoon. Do not allow the water to boil, because the custard will curdle. Remove from the fire, add the soaked gelatine to the custard, stir until it is dissolved, and set the mixture in a cold place. When slightly thickened, stir in the vanilla and one-half of the cocoanut, then fold in stiffly beaten egg whites. Pour into a baked pie shell and sprinkle the remaining cocoanut on top. Set in the refrigerator for 2 to 3 hours before serving.

South Florida Freeze

6 cups grated cocoanut (2 large co-
　coanuts) yields 4¼ cups ex-
　tracted cocoanut milk
½ teaspoon vanilla

3½ cups boiling water
⅞ cup cocoanut water
1⅛ cups sugar

Pour the boiling water over the grated cocoanut and allow to stand 15 minutes. Strain through a double thickness of cheesecloth, squeezing out as much of the milk as possible. Add the cocoanut water, sugar and vanilla to the extracted cocoanut milk, and stir until the sugar is dissolved. Freeze in an ice-cream freezer, using 8 parts of ice to 1 part of ice cream salt.

Grated cocoanut may be served over the frozen mixture.

Cocoanut-Sweet Potato Pie

1 cup shredded cocoanut
1½ cups mashed sweet potatoes
¾ cup sugar
¾ cup rich milk
½ cup water

½ teaspoon cinnamon
½ teaspoon allspice
2 tablespoons melted butter
2 eggs (slightly beaten)

Mix the above ingredients and pour into a pan lined with unbaked pastry.

Appendix
The Following Recipes Were Furnished Us by the
FLORIDA ADVERTISING ASSOCIATION
WINTER HAVEN

GRAPEFRUIT CREAM SHERBET

1 tablespoon gelatin	2 cups orange juice
½ cup cold water	1½ cups grapefruit juice
1½ cups sugar	1 pint cream or evaporated milk
1½ cups boiling water	½ cup powdered sugar
Grated rind of 1 grapefruit	Few grains salt
2 eggs	

Soak gelatine in cold water for five minutes. Dissolve gelatine and 1½ cups sugar in boiling water. Add grapefruit rind, juice and orange juice. Place in mold next to ice, or in tray of your quick freezer and harden to mush. Beat cream until stiff, add ½ cup sugar and salt. Separate yolks from whites. Beat yolks until foaming and whites until stiff. Combine, add to cream. Fold into the hardened mixture. Return to freezer or top of ice. Stir this mixture twice during the freezing process.

GRAPEFRUIT CREME DELIGHT

Heat one cup of thin cream with a few grains of salt and add the yolk of one egg beaten with three tablespoons of sugar. Remove from fire as soon as the cream has thickened slightly and add while hot, one tablespoon of finely grated grapefruit rind. Allow it to cool and fold in one cup of double cream whipped solid, three-quarters of a cup of crushed macaroon crumbs, and the juice of one grapefruit. Freeze slowly.

MARMALADE

2 oranges	2 lemons	Sugar, water

First slice fruit as thin as possible, saving seeds. After slicing fruit, measure it carefully, and add exactly as much water as fruit. Pour water over fruit, and let stand forty-eight hours. Then bring to boil and boil for an hour. Boil seeds up in water. Strain them out, and add water in which they cooked, to fruit. The seeds contain the pectin which causes the jelling process. After boiling let it stand over night. Next day boil again, but add equal amount of sugar as you have fruit and water. Boil until thickens to your fancy. Stir several times while it is standing, so each piece of fruit has an equal chance to soften.

CANDIED GRAPEFRUIT PEEL

Rinds of 3 grapefruits	3 cups sugar
Water	

Cut rind lengthwise from grapefruit and cut in strips ¼-in. wide. Cover in cold water for several hours. Drain. Cover again in cold water and bring to a boiling point. Drain. Repeat this process once again to remove any bitterness from the fruit when done. Cover with water, add sugar to equal the rind, and cook until clear. If sirup becomes too thick before rind is clear, add hot water to the same amount of original thickness. When clear, drain and dip in granulated sugar. Do this for three successive days. Pack in air-tight containers.

BITTER ORANGE MARMALADE

1 grapefruit	2 oranges
1 lemon	¼ cup lemon juice

Slice the unpeeled fruit very thin. Add three times as much water as fruit. Boil 20 minutes. Measure, bring to boiling point. Add ¾ cup sugar for each cup of fruit. Boil 25 minutes or until it gives the jelly test. Just before removing from fire, add ¼ cup lemon juice. Pour into sterilized glasses; cover with paraffin when cold.

ELOISE MUFFINS

Sweeten and drain grapefruit pulp. Cream ½ cup shortening, add ½ cup sugar. Beat 2 eggs—add to above mixture. Add 1 cup milk. Sift 2 teaspoons baking powder with 3 cups flour and 1 teaspoon salt. Add ¼ teaspoon baking soda to 1 cup grapefruit pulp. Add to first mixture. Put in muffin tins. Bake ½ hour at 350 degrees. Makes about 16.

UPSIDE DOWN CAKE

½ lb. butter	2 tablespoons baking powder
1½ cups sugar	2½ cups pastry flour
3 eggs	1 cup grapefruit juice

Grease pan thickly with butter. Place three cups grapefruit pulp in pan, with one cup brown sugar. Mix batter in the usual way and pour over the grapefruit in pan. Bake in moderate oven for about fifty minutes. May be served with whipped cream if desired.

SUNSHINE CAKE

4 egg yolks	1 cup sugar
½ cup canned grapefruit juice	1 cup flour
1 teaspoon baking powder	Few grains salt

Beat the egg yolks until thick. Add the sugar and continue beating. Add the grapefruit juice, then fold in the beaten egg whites. Sift the flour with the baking powder and few grains of salt. Fold in carefully with the first mixture. Bake in an ungreased tube pan in slow oven, 325°, for fifty to sixty minutes. Turn upside down and let cool and it will pull itself away from the sides of the pan. Ice with a boiled icing in which grapefruit juice has been substituted for water, or add confectioner's sugar and a little melted butter to the juice until the right consistency to spread.

GRAPEFRUIT SNOW PUDDING

Sprinkle one tablespoon of gelatine in one-fourth cup cold water. Soak for five minutes or add immediately according to directions on the package, to one-fourth cup boiling water, one-fourth cup orange juice, one tablespoon lemon juice and three-fourths cup grapefruit hearts; stir until dissolved. When the jelly cools and begins to thicken, beat until frothy and fold in the stiffly beaten egg whites of two eggs. Chill in individual molds and at serving time turn out and garnish with a few slices of grapefruit.

GRAPEFRUIT SURPRISE

1 tablespoon mayonnaise	Grenadine
Lettuce	Pears
Strawberries	Lemon juice
Grapefruit	

Arrange a cup of lettuce on each salad plate. Then arrange alternate sections of grapefruit and pears. Place a strawberry tip up, at the outer edge of each section. Add a little lemon juice and grenadine to the mayonnaise to make of consistency to pipe with pastry tube. Pipe between sections of grapefruit and pears with the grenadine mayonnaise.

AVOCADO CITRUS SALAD

Cut a peeled avocado into rather thin slices crosswise, then cut each slice again once or twice the other way. Arrange on crisp leaves of lettuce alternately with segments of orange and grapefruit from which all the skin has been removed. Garnish with strips of pimento and serve with French dressing made with lemon juice, and only a little oil.

GRAPEFRUIT ROSE

Cut a grapefruit in two, take out all the sections, skin them and cut in small pieces. Trim the edges of the hollow halves in pointed scallops. Combine the cut fruit with bits of orange, avocado pear, chipped apple or pear and put the mixture into the trimmed grapefruit skins. Garnish with maraschino cherry or preserved ginger, also with a sprig of water cress and a little dab of mayonnaise.

FRUIT SALAD ASPIC

2 tablespoons gelatine
2 cups hot water
2 oranges
1 grapefruit, grapes, canned peaches and pears

½ cup cold water
1¼ cups sugar
1 lemon

Soften the gelatine in cold water and dissolve in hot water. In place of 1 cup of the water a cup of fruit juice may be used if desired. Add the sugar and stir until dissolved. Add the juice of oranges and lemon. When the mixture begins to thicken, add sections of grapefruit, the grapes with seeds removed, and halves of canned peaches and pears. Turn the mixture into a mold. If desired, clear aspic may be poured into a ring mold and the fruit piled in the center of the ring when the jelly is unmolded.

GRAPEFRUIT AND CHEESE SALAD

Peel a grapefruit, separate the sections, skin them and keep them whole. Slice and peel a small ripe pineapple, cut into little cubes and arrange these on crisp lettuce leaves.

Surround with grapefruit sections, petal fashion. Place a piece of roquefort, gruyere, brie or cream cheese on the pineapple. Garnish with a strip of pimento. Serve with French dressing.

CRABMEAT AND GRAPEFRUIT SALAD

One pound of crab meat (fresh preferred), 1 can grapefruit, drained. Marinate crabmeat in French dressing. Mix crabmeat and grapefruit together, adding a small amount of mayonnaise, a few capers, and salt and pepper to taste. Lay on lettuce hearts and top with mayonnaise sprinkled with paprika.

SALAD DRESSING

1 teaspoon powdered sugar
¼ teaspoon paprika
2 tablespoons vinegar
1 cup oil

1 teaspoon salt
¼ teaspoon mustard
¼ cup evaporated milk
2 tablespoons evaporated milk

Oil and milk should be cold. Measure sugar, salt, mustard, paprika, and the one-quarter cup evaporated milk into a cold bowl. Beat well, add one-quarter cup oil, a little at a time, then remainder of oil and vinegar alternately, beating well after each addition. Add the two tablespoons evaporated milk and beat again thorouhgly.

GRAPEFRUIT SALAD

Peel two grapefruit, cutting away the white skin. Remove pulp, keeping each section whole. Arrange five sections of the fruit like the petals of a daisy on leaves of crisp romaine or lettuce. Place a teaspoon of grated American cheese around the inner points of the fruit sections to carry out the idea of the flower. Serve with French dressing.

GRAPEFRUIT COMBINATION SALAD

3 fresh grapefruit
½ pint cream
1 large can unsliced pears
12 marshmallows

1 package cream cheese
½ can Queen Anne cherries
1 small can crushed pineapple

Cut the marshmallows in fourths with wet scissors and soak them over night in the cream. In the morning whip them together and crumble in the cream cheese, which should have been standing at room temperature for several hours in order to soften. Beat the mixture again until smooth and creamy. Just before the meal arrange crisp lettuce on the plates and place a chilled, drained pear, hollow side up, in the center of each. Around each pear arrange sections of grapefruit in the form of a flower. Pile the chilled, drained cherries in the center of the pear and over the salad pour the dressing. Sprinkle a little drained pineapple over this and offer up very chilly. This will serve eight.

APPETIZER SALAD IN GRAPEFRUIT BASKETS

Cut the grapefruit in two and make a four-section handled basket from each half in the following manner: Insert two toothpicks near cut edge opposite each other. From ¼ in. on each side of toothpick, cut through skin around the grapefruit ¼ in. from top of cut surface. Remove pulp from this cut part so that the two strips of peel can be tied together to form basket handle.

SURPRISE SUNDAE

Take large sweet potatoes and bake until pulp is soft. Cut in halves and scoop out pulp. Mix each half individually. Mix pulp with ¼ teaspoon butter and ¼ teaspoon confectioner's sugar and ½ teaspoon grapefruit rind grated fine. Put back in sweet potato shell and top with whipped cream and sprinkle finely grated grapefruit rind on top of whipped cream.

CASSEROLE OF YAMS AND GRAPEFRUIT

1 lb. of yams (red sweet potato)	2 tablespoons cream
½ teaspoon salt	¼ teaspoon nutmeg
2 tablespoons butter	Grapefruit sections

Wash yams, cut off ends, and boil until tender in salted water, 1 teaspoon to one quart of water. Peel and mash fine with ½ teaspoon salt, the nutmeg, cream and butter. Put in buttered pyrex casserole. Over the top arrange grapefruit sections (free from seeds and white skin) pinwheel design, radiating from center. Dot with butter and sprinkle granulated sugar over all just before heating to serve. This can be prepared in the morning or even the day before. Just cover and set in your refrigerator until time to reheat. Leave in the oven just long enough to heat thoroughly and melt the sugar on top.

GRAPEFRUIT A LA GRILLE

Cut each grapefruit in half, core and remove the seeds. Sprinkle one tablespoon brown sugar over the top of each half. Place three cherries in the center and add a little of the juice. Preheat the oven broiler for about ten minutes. Place the grapefruit under the flame for seven or ten minutes. The sugar will melt and spread to give the grapefruit a lovely browned surface, and a delightful new flavor.

Remove all membrane from sections of chilled grapefruit, arranging the sections in a wheel on a dessert plate, then pouring hot chocolate sauce over the fruit just before serving. Maraschino juice used to sweeten grapefruit served in the shell imparts a delicate color and flavor. No sugar is needed in this case. Try crushed maple sugar or honey for sweetening instead of sugar.

With a curved grapefruit knife, remove the pulp, leaving four of the white membrane divisions as partitions to form equal sized sections. Place a different salad or appetizer in each of the four sections. Tuna fish, celery, cucumber and a tiny bit of green pepper mixed with mayonnaise could be used for one; radish roses in another; celery curls or olives, green and ripe, in a third. In fourth section place diced grapefruit pulp and avocado which has been marinated with French dressing. Serve on salad plate as first course of a luncheon or dinner. Garnish top of partitions and center with mayonnaise forced through pastry bag.

CAUGIN

Scoop all meat from bright, clear-skinned grapefruit halves. Scallop the edges. Dice alligator pear, orange and grapefruit. Pile into grapefruit baskets. Sprinkle top with a little finely chopped canton ginger and green pepper. Place on pale glass plate, garnish with water cress. Serve with mayonnaise flavored with a little minced ginger and cognac.

DREAM BOATS

One banana for each person served. Cut in two lengthwise and arrange both sections on crisp lettuce.

½ cup grapefruit pulp   ½ cup white grapes
½ cup orange pulp   Few shredded nut meats

Remainder of banana pulp that has been scooped out to make boats. Moisten with French dressing and place mixture with banana boats, garnishing with sliced maraschino cherries, and serve with hot crackers.

SALAD

½ cup diced apple   ½ cup diced celery
2 cups grapefruit   1 cup smoked salmon
Desired amount of water cress.

Season well and mix with French dressing or mayonnaise.

GRAPEFRUIT-ROQUEFORT SALAD

Grapefruit   Roquefort cheese
French dressing   Cress
Green pepper, minced or in thin strips

Peel grapefruit and slice thinly across; cut in half again cross wise, rejecting all seeds; allow 2 slices for portion. Arrange on cress-covered plates.

Pour over dressing, in which Roquefort cheese has been smoothly mashed. Garnish with minced pepper or pepper strips.

FLORIDA SALAD

1 grapefruit   1 Spanish onion
French dressing   Lettuce

Buy solid grapefruits. Peel and slice in round slices. Slice onion. Lay slices of grapefruit on bed of lettuce, and lay slice of onion on grapefruit and strip of pimento. Pour over it the French dressing.

GRAPEFRUIT SHRIMP SALAD

1 cup grapefruit section, cut in pieces   1 cup shrimp, cut in pieces
⅓ cup cucumber, diced   ¾ cup celery, diced
⅓ cup mayonnaise   Lettuce, pimento

Add ingredients in order given. Chill in refrigerator and serve on crisp lettuce. Garnish with small pimento strips. This makes six servings.

BRAZIL NUT SALAD

1 cup grapefruit   1 package cream cheese
¼ cup Brazil nuts   Lettuce
Cream mayonnaise or French dressing.

Make cheese into little balls and roll in coarsely chopped nuts. Drain juice from can of grapefruit. Arrange grapefruit sections and three cheese balls to a serving on cup shaped lettuce leaves. In center put a pasteurized date (stuffed with date-cheese mixture). Cover with dressing and sprinkle with chopped nutmeats. Other nutmeats may be substituted for Brazil nuts. Six servings.

FRUIT SALAD

2/3 cup diced pineapple   ½ cup seeded white cherries
½ cup grapefruit   ⅓ cup red cherries

Mix and chill ingredients. Drain juices and arrange fruit on lettuce and top with salad dressing.

WASHINGTON GRAPEFRUIT SALAD

Peel and remove the outer skin of the grapefruit. Arrange sections of the grapefruit on lettuce leaves, and between each section place red cherries. Top with a generous amount of mayonnaise.

GRAPEFRUIT SALAD

Dissolve 2 packages lemon jelly in 2 cups boiling water and cool. Add ¼ cup lemon juice and the juice from one No. 2 can grapefruit. Set away to chill. Chill, then peel 1 large avocado and cut in small cubes and arrange in bottom of 1 large or 8 to 10 small molds. Dust lightly with salt. Sprinkle over ¼ cup blanched, chopped almonds, then pour over the thickened jelly and set away to harden. Unmold on lettuce and garnish with the grapefruit sections and mayonnaise. Serves 8 to 10.

GRAPEFRUIT PONCE DE LEON

¾ cup grapefruit juice   ¼ cup honey

Mix grapefruit and honey. Place in refrigerator over night. Serve.

GRAPEFRUIT CUP

2 cups grapefruit juice	2 cups orange juice
¾ cup powdered sugar	1 bottle ginger ale
¼ cup maraschino juice	8 to 10 Maraschino cherries
1 orange sliced thin	1 banana sliced thin

Mix and serve over cracked or cubed ice. Garnish with sliced fruit.

FLORIDA SPECIAL SALAD

2 grapefruits	1 alligator pear
Romaine salad	2 pimentos
2 oranges	French dressing

Peel fruit, separate segments. Slice alligator pear in thin slices. Slice pimentos in narrow strips. Arrange the fruit alternately on romaine leaves, decorating with strips of pimento. Serve with French dressing.

FRENCH DRESSING

⅓ cup grapefruit juice	¾-1 cup olive oil
1 teaspoon salt	1 teaspoon sugar
¼ teaspoon paprika	

Blend seasoning with olive oil, add grapefruit juice. Pour into a bottle, shake well before using. Will keep indefinitely in refrigerator.

ST. PATRICK'S DAY MINT SALAD

1 package lily white mint gelatine	¾ cup boiling water
1 cup grapefruit juice	Segments of 1 grapefruit
Maraschino cherries	½ cup canned pineapple, cut in
Water cress	segments

Dissolve gelatine in boiling water, scald grapefruit juice. Chill. Arrange grapefruit sections in mold. When gelatine is slightly thickened, turn some into mold, taking care not to move the fruit. Chill. Add more fruit and liquid. Unmold on water cress. Serve with mayonnaise dressing.

GRAPEFRUIT WHIP

⅓ cup grapefruit pulp	1¼ cups chopped nutmeats
⅓ cup powdered sugar	3 tablespoons marshmallow creme
2 tablespoons currant jelly	3 Maraschino cherries, diced
1 egg white	

Combine and beat grapefruit pulp, sugar, jelly, marshmallow creme, nuts and cherries. Whip white until dry and stiff, and fold in first mixture. Serve immediately in sherbet glasses, garnishing top with whole Maraschino cherry. Lady fingers, sponge cake or vanilla wafers may be served with it or the whip laid in portions on each cake.

GRAPEFRUIT MINT SALAD

1 tablespoon gelatine
1½ cups canned grapefruit juice
3 tablespoons sirup from cherries

2 tablespoons cold water
2 tablespoons sugar
8 green mint cherries

Soak gelatine in cold water. Add grapefruit juice heated to the boiling point, sugar and sirup from the cherries. Stir until gelatine and sugar are dissolved. When the mixture begins to thicken add the cherries finely minced and pour into molds. Serve with mayonnaise. This makes six servings.

GRAPEFRUIT BOX SALAD

1 cup diced grapefruit pulp
½ cup seeded white cherries
½ cup seeded red cherries
½ cup diced marshmallows

½ cup nutmeats
Grapefruit mayonnaise
Square saltines

Mix ingredients. Add dressing. Arrange on lettuce-covered plates. Place 4 saltines like a box around salad, and tie in shape with narrow ribbon to match preferred color scheme.

GRAPEFRUIT SALAD DRESSING

1 cup salad oil
Dash of pepper
⅓ cup grapefruit juice

¾ teaspoon salt
½ teaspoon sugar

Mix all ingredients and shake in a covered bottle until thick.

CAKES
GRAPEFRUIT QUICK SHORTCAKE

Sections grapefruit
Sections canned peaches
4 tablespoons powdered sugar
Maraschino cherries

4 tablespoons shredded cocoanut
½ cup heavy cream
Loaf sponge cake

Use individual plates and arrange 1 slice of cake on each plate. Allow 2 sections grapefruit and 2 sections peach to each serving. Arrange fruits alternately in each of the four corners of cake slice. Sprinkle fruits with sugar and shredded cocoanut. Pile sweetened whipped cream in center space and top with Maraschino garnish. (Canned apricots and pears and thin sections of canned pineapple can be similarly used with grapefruit sections.)

BAKED GRAPEFRUIT SOUFFLE

½ cup grapefruit pulp
½ cup orange pulp
2 egg whites

1 cup sugar
1 teaspoon flour
⅛ teaspoon salt

Rub fruit pulp through sieve; add sugar, butter, salt and heat. Fold stiffly beaten whites into hot fruit pulp. Fill greased baking dish or small molds three-quarters full of mixture and set in a pan of hot water. Bake in slow oven about 25 minutes until firm. Serve with whipped cream or with grapefruit sauce.

GRAPEFRUIT SOUFFLE

1 cup milk
½ cup cut up grapefruit sections
3 tablespoons orange juice
½ cup sugar
½ tablespoon vanilla

4 tablespoons flour
4 tablespoons butter
1 tablespoon lemon juice
Grated rind of ½ orange

Make a white sauce of the flour, butter and milk. Cool. Add the rest of the ingredients except the egg whites. Beat these very stiff and fold in last. Turn into a buttered baking dish and bake in a moderately slow oven about one hour. A fluffy grapefruit souffle may be offered to the most sophisticated of diners.

PIES
GRAPEFRUIT MERINGUE PIE

1 cup sugar	2 tablespoons flour
Juice ½ Florida grapefruit	¼ tablespoon melted butter
1 cup boiling water	3 to 6 tablespoons sugar for meringue

Mix flour, sugar and salt, and add boiling water gradually, stirring constantly. Add butter and cook 15 minutes over hot water. Add grapefruit juice and beaten yolks of eggs, stirring the eggs in quickly. Take from the fire. Cool and turn into a baked crust. Cover with a meringue made from the stiffly beaten egg whites and sugar. Brown in a slow oven.

CINNAMON TOAST PIE

Take four slices of toast, and butter and sprinkle with cinnamon. Break into pieces and line a pie plate. Cut grapefruit into small pieces, sprinkle with sugar and put on top of toast. Dot with butter. Beat whites of two eggs with 6 tablespoons of sugar and spread on top of grapefruit. Bake in oven until whites are golden brown.

CINNAMON FRUIT TOAST

6 slices bread	1 egg
¼ cup grapefruit juice	1 cup sugar
Grated rind of grapefruit	2 slices oranges
Powdered sugar	

Beat egg with lemon and grapefruit juice until well blended, then add sugar that has been mixed with the grated grapefruit rind and beat well. Cut circles from the bread slices and dip in the egg mixture. Fry on a buttered pan until golden brown on both sides. Cover with orange slices, sift with powdered sugar and serve immediately. (To prepare oranges, peel, taking with it all the white membrane. With a thin, sharp knife, cut the orange into thin strips lengthwise.)

HAM AND GRAPEFRUIT

Peel and remove the sections from a large seedless grapefruit. Cut the sections in halves lengthwise, then place them over the top of the almost-cooked ham. Sprinkle a thin layer of brown sugar over the fruit and finish cooking the ham.

GRAPEFRUIT WITH FISH

Soak the fish in grapefruit juice ten or fifteen minutes before being cooked. The tart juice will add a tang that counteracts the blandness of fish and that will give a distinguished flavor.

V — The Truth About Diet

First See That Your Health Is Good Before
Starting on Reducing Diet

FOR REDUCING WEIGHT

By Dr. Morris Fishbein, Editor

Journal of American Medical Association, and of *Hygeia,* the Health Magazine

(Used with permission of Dr. Morris Fishbein)

The first essential in dieting is that you be in good health before you reduce. If your doctor gives his approval, you can lose about two pounds a week by taking an arrangement of food that provides about 1200 or 1400 calories a day.

Here is one day's menu of 1200 calories, that includes all your body needs in the way of proteins, carbohydrates, fats, mineral salts, and vitamins:

Breakfast: One-half orange, two eggs, one thin piece dry toast, coffee sweetened with saccharin, two tablespoonfuls of thin cream, and one small cube of butter.

Lunch: Slice of lean meat, two tablespoonfuls peas or string beans, one-half head lettuce with a little French dressing.

Dinner: Clear bouillon, two slices lean meat, spinach or carrots, one-half head lettuce with French dressing, one-half orange, tea sweetened with saccharin, one-fourth of a cup of milk, a thin slice of bread toast, and a small cube of butter.

If there is any food on the list that you do not like it is easy to substitute. One-half grapefruit can be substituted for the orange; an egg may be taken instead of the meat; cucumbers, radishes, asparagus, turnips, cabbage, spinach, or watercress may be used as alternate vegetables; or several may be taken at one time to make up a salad.

Occasionally, berries or tomato may be substituted for the orange or the grapefruit.

Here is another menu developed by a medical authority. It contains a little over 1000 calories, and if you will eat just these foods and no others and carry on your normal work, you will lose from two to two and one-half pounds a week. If you do extra work or take more exercise, you will lose more.

Breakfast: Two small oranges or one large one, one egg, one slice toasted bread (thin), one small square butter, one glass skim milk, one cup tea or coffee, clear.

Luncheon or dinner: One cup consomme, one medium slice roast beef, three heaping tablespoons spinach, one salad containing eight stalks of asparagus on two leaves of lettuce, with vinegar; six heaping tablespoonfuls of sliced peaches, one glass skim milk, one cup clear tea.

Supper: Three heaping tablespoonfuls of cottage cheese, three heaping tablespoonfuls of cauliflower, one baked tomato, one-third head lettuce with lemon juice or vinegar, six heaping tablespoonfuls of red raspberries, one glass skim milk, one cup clear tea.

"This diet contains," you may insist, "twice as much food as I usually eat." But this observation is faulty. The list contains a variety of ingredients, but all are chosen with exact knowledge of what they provide in the way of calories and essential food substances.

Wrong selection of food, a sweet tooth, and lack of sufficient exercise, warns a great nutrition specialist, are the primary reasons for reducing diets.

Remember that Americans consume from five to ten times as much sugar per person per day as do people abroad. This sugar is not all taken as such, but usually is distributed through a wide variety of foods.

The average stewed tomatoes or other vegetables served in a restaurant would hardly be eatable without considerable seasoning. When you are reducing, you must avoid, particularly, rich salad dressing. sugar, custards, candies, cakes, pies, rich gravies, fat fish, fat meats, nuts, cream, fried foods, or creamed soups.

Here is a diet that contains about 1016 calories. It provides all the essential food substances. On this diet you may lose from two to three pounds a week if you keep up your ordinary work.

Remember, it is not safe to reduce more rapidly.

Breakfast: One-half grapefruit, one tablespoonful cream, one egg, one slice bread, one medium serving puffed rice or similar cereal, one slice thin toast and one small square butter.

Luncheon or dinner: One cup plain broth, one broiled trout or other fish, three heaping tablespoonfuls new peas, salad containing one tomato and two leaves of lettuce with vinegar or lemon, one-half cantaloupe or grapefruit, one glass skim milk, one cup clear tea or coffee.

Supper: Three slices white meat of chicken, three slices of egg plant, three heaping tablespoonfuls cream squash, four stalks celery hearts, one cup clear tea, one glass skim milk, one banana.

FOR ADDING WEIGHT

If you are seriously underweight you should eat food containing 4000 to 5000 calories each day. The carbohydrate or sugar content of such a diet should represent about 2000 calories; proteins, approximately 120 grams.

Chief weight-building substances in the diet are milk, cream, butter, bacon, breads, and vegetables which offer plenty of calories, such as peas, lima beans, rice, macaroni and spaghetti. In addition, foods especially rich in carbohydrates such as malted milk, dry milk, and olive oil may prove helpful.

Regular meals may be supplemented by extra food eaten at 10:30 in the morning, 4 in the afternoon and 9:30 in the evening.

Foods with high water or roughage content should, of course, be omitted or used sparingly. These include such products as asparagus, bouillon, cauliflower, cucumbers, sauerkraut, tomatoes, radishes, celery, wax beans, beets, carrots, parsnips, lettuce, onions, pumpkins, turnips, and squash.

Here is a menu that will be of value in helping you to gain weight:

Breakfast: Chilled grapefruit with honey or grenadine, farina with dates or raisins, cream and sugar, jelly omelet, fatty bacon, toast and jam, coffee with cream, sugar.

Luncheon: Tomatoes stuffed with minced lamb, baked spaghetti with cheese, jellied vegetable salad, French or Russian dressing, melba toast, fruit, cake or fruit pie, hot chocolate.

Dinner: Cream of tomato soup, cheese crackers, broiled tenderloin steak, baked potato balls rolled in parsley and butter, buttered parsnips, buttered lima beans, hard rolls, butter, cream tapioca with dates, coffee with cream, sugar.

Another good weight-building menu:

Breakfast: Bananas and cream, cooked cereal with cream, honey or sugar, French toast, maple syrup, hot chocolate.

Luncheon: Baked ham with sauteed pineapple rings, scalloped asparagus, bread, butter, jellied dates with hard sauce, milk.

Dinner: Barley vegetable soup, broiled mackerel or halibut steak with egg sauce, creamed celery, baked potato with butter, baked cauliflower with cheese, tomato or vegetable salad with mayonnaise, gluten bread and butter, cottage pudding with hot lemon sauce, or caramel custard pudding, coffee with cream, sugar.

The person who wants to gain weight will, of course, indulge moderately in exercise, such as walking and golf, but avoid exhausting or strenuous exercise.

Persons who wish to gain weight may omit extra water between meals. Foods taken will probably supply necessary water.

VI—The Body Needs and Menus to Meet the Needs

The body needs that make proper food selection necessary are as follows: 1. Energy. 2. Building and repairing of tissues. 3. Regulation of various body processes. 4. Promotion of health and growth. All materials that help the body to meet these four needs are now accepted as "foods." In planning a diet for a family it is necessary to understand at least the basic needs.

1. Energy. Walking, standing, hand work, breathing, digestion, heart beats, and all other body processes require energy, all of which must be supplied by food—the right kind of food. The activity, size and age of the body as well as the climate decide the amount of food to be consumed for this purpose.

Energy Foods:

Starch and Sugar—Cereals, macaroni, spaghetti, bread, potatoes, corn, beans, rice, sirups, cane sugar and fruit and a number of root VEGETABLES.

Fats—Butter, cream, vegetable and animal oils, nuts.

Calories Needed—About 2,200 calories (fats, starches and sugar) daily for the average person.

2. Building and Repair. There must be constant building to repair waste, to promote growth, and to strengthen bone and muscle and other body tissues (in case of the young). No one food nor class of foods supplies all the needed materials.

Building Foods:

Protein—Milk, lean meat, eggs, cheese, fish, nuts, whole cereals, dried peas and beans and other VEGETABLE foods.

Minerals—(Builders and regulators—they enter into the tissues and fluids, regulate heart action, and assist in coagulating blood. Lime builds bones, teeth. Iron is needed for blood. Phosphorus is needed everywhere.)

FRUITS AND VEGETABLES; milk.

Water—(Water forms a part of every living cell.)

Calories Needed—250 to 300 calories daily.

3. Regulation. The human body with its constant heart beat, its steady circulation, a digestive tract that receives food three times daily, takes it slowly into the body, eliminates the useless material, and, at the same time, delivers to the body, by way of blood circulation, that portion of the food needed by the body, requires smooth, accurate regulation if the processes are going on well for from 40 to 80 years. If the intricate organs working out a master-piece of cooperation do not receive the proper foods then defects and pains result.

Regulation Foods:

Minerals—FRUITS AND VEGETABLES and milk.

Bulk or Fiber—FRUITS AND VEGETABLES, starch and the bran of grains, and water.

Vitamins—FRUITS AND VEGETABLES, milk, fish, oil.

4. Growth and Health—Vitamins. By animal feeding experiments scientists have learned, without a doubt, that natural foods contain certain constituents which are essential for health and nutrition but present in such minute traces as to escape detection by ordinary methods. This group of elusive food constituents is known as vitamins. Their importance in normal nutrition and in preventive medicine is becoming more and more evident with each succeeding year. It is not discouraging that mistakes have been made, old knowledge cast aside for the new, theories changed. As time goes on we shall know more. The question is not "Do I believe in vitamins?" but "where can I get vitamins?" The answer may at least be partially answered as follows:

FRUITS AND VEGETABLES.

Growth and Health Foods:

Vitamin A (increases resistance to infection)—Green and yellow vegetables. All green vegetables are richer in vitamin A than are white vegetables. Green-leaf lettuce is richer than white leaves, green asparagus than the bleached, young, green cabbage than the headed, and probably green string beans than the wax beans. Green peas, "greens" (turnip greens), collards, kale. spinach, beet greens are rich in vitamin A. Broccoli and Brussels sprouts probably take precedence over cauliflower and cabbage. Florida's green-leaf lettuce, endive and green peppers are probably very much richer in vitamin A than the white lettuce shipped into the state. Yellow vegetables, such as yellow squash, carrots, rutabagas, deep yellow sweet potatoes (the Southerner's delight), and yellow corn are rich sources of vitamin A. as are also yellow fruits, such as oranges, tangerines, satsumas, papayas. Other fruits having vitamin A in generous amount are tomatoes.

Vitamin C—Protects teeth. Tomatoes, oranges, strawberries, cabbage, and all CITRUS FRUITS and pineapple are good sources.

Vitamin D (found in fats. Anti-rachitic)—There seems to be a general opinion that vitamin D is not stored to any great extent in vegetables grown in northern climates. Vegetables and oranges have been artificially irradiated. It is more than likely true that vegetables and fruits grown in Florida's sunshine and allowed to mature thoroughly in the sun do contain anti-rachitic power, vitamin D. (Requests have been made for experimental work along this line and it is hoped that in the near future there will be definite information on the subject.)

Vitamin E—Prevents sterility. The best sources are lettuce leaves, and other green leaves.

Vitamin F—Promotes appetite, prevents nervousness. Legumes are a good source of vitamin F.

Vitamin G—Prevents pellagra. Fresh vegetables, of the leafy type particularly, and tomatoes and bananas.

"The greatest lack in the American diet is in minerals and in vitamins," says Dr. Louise Stanley, Director Home Economics Bureau, U. S. Department of Agriculture. FRESH FRUITS, VEGETABLES and MILK are the foods which form the surest source of all minerals and vitamins.

A Few Suggestions Concerning Florida Menus

Purpose:

To supplement a general diet with a sufficient supply of fresh or canned FLORIDA FRUITS AND VEGETABLES.

Key:

Two vegetables, one green (in season) every day.

A raw vegetable or a fruit every day.[1]

A generous amount of roots, tubers and pod vegetables.

Milk, eggs, meat, starches and accessories to complete the menu.

Points to Remember:

1. Fruits supply sugar in nature's own form and combinations.
2. Potatoes and root vegetables help to take the place of bread.
3. Vegetables supply protein in small amounts but of good quality.
4. Nuts partake of the nature of meats and fats.
5. "In season" foods are more economical than "out of season" products.
6. Foods produced locally cost less than products from other sections.
7. Simple, natural foods, prepared to hold the texture, flavor and nutritive value, are most wholesome, attractive and economical.
8. Vegetable plate:

   Taste—One mild in flavor, one pronounced, one acid or relish.

   Texture—One boiled or steamed.
   One "crispy."
   One in sauce.
   One raw.

   Protein—Beans or peas.
   One served with egg, milk, or cheese.

   Color—One or two bright colors—beets, carrots, tomato squash, rutabaga; one green; never serve all white.

[1]Canned grapefruit, tomatoes, strawberries, are good substitutes in food value for the fresh fruit.

Group Varieties of Vegetables

Too often in meal planning no distinction is made as to varieties of groups of vegetables. There are four distinct types considered from a nutritive standpoint—Pods, Roots, Tubers and Leaves.

POD VEGETABLES

This is the legume group. These vegetables are especially rich in protein and are, therefore, partial substitutes for meat in the diet. In the fresh stage they are fairly rich in vitamin B. They are good source of phosphorus, and a fair source of iron. They are alkaline in their reaction and have this advantage over other protein foods. Peas and lima beans are somewhat similar in food value. String beans or snap beans are more like green leaves. Their mature seeds are similar to peas.

ROOT VEGETABLES

This group is not outstanding in food value but it has a place as a group in adding variety and attractiveness and in supplementing more concentrated foods. Carrots, especially raw carrots, are a good source of vitamin, as are also beets and rutabagas. Kohl-rabi is a splendid source of phosphorus, calcium and protein.

TUBERS

This group is made up of the vegetables rich in carbohydrates, such as white and sweet potato and is, therefore, an important source of energy. The sweet potato is especially rich in vitamin A. White potato has vitamin B and, if properly cooked, has a mineral value. It is a good plan to alternate the use of these two potatoes and to allow them to help take the place of bread and rice as the potatoes have an excess of base over acid. Potatoes should never form the basis of a diet. They are lacking in calcium.

GREEN LEAVES

This group has two types, the thick leaves, such as cabbage, onion, cauliflower, lettuce, and the thin leaves, such as turnip greens, spinach, mustard. The mineral, vitamin, protein and roughage values have been previously discussed.

Suggested Menus

Breakfast
Papaya with Lime
Soft-cooked Eggs   Toast with Butter
Sugar and Cream for Coffee
or
Milk to Drink

Lunch
Avocado Salad with Lettuce
Bread and Butter
Milk or Lemonade

Dinner
Vegetable Soup (cream)
Chicken or Meat
Sweet Potato, baked   Butter
Stewed Okra   Green Beans
Lemon Pie

Breakfast
Mango or Peach with Cream
Bacon   Hot Muffin
Milk or Coffee

Lunch
Cottage Cheese Salad with Escarole
Marmalade   Bread and Butter
Fruit Juice

Dinner
Fruit Cup
Baked Fish with Tomato and
Pepper Sauce
Green Beans   Baked Potato
Blueberry Pie

Breakfast
Bananas with Orange Juice
Eggs Scrambled in Thin Cream
Corn Muffins and Butter
Milks or Coffee

Lunch
Vegetable Stew
Bread and Butter   Celery
Fruit Pudding

Dinner
Smothered Chicken with Plum Jelly
Steamed Chard   Baked Squash
Lettuce and Tomato Salad

Breakfast
Grapefruit
Bacon   Toast   Pineapple Jam
Milk or Coffee

Lunch
Fruit Salad with Cheese Toast
Celery   Pecans

Dinner
Turnips and Turnip Greens
with Bacon
Green Pepper and Tomato Salad
Corn Muffins

Breakfast
Orange Juice (undiluted)
Waffles   Stewed Guavas
Milk or Coffee

Lunch
Fish Chowder
Cabbage Salad with Grated Carrot
Toast with Butter
Citrus Marmalade

Dinner
(Vegetable Plate)
Beets   Green Beans
Yellow Squash or Carrots
Okra   Cole Slaw
Corn Sticks   Butter
Spiced Plums   Peanut Cookies

Breakfast
Blueberries with Orange Juice
Muffins
Scrambled Eggs with Bacon

Lunch
Cheese with Stewed or Fresh Figs
Brown Bread   Milk
Grapefruit

Dinner
Broiled Steak   Steamed Onions
Sliced Tomatoes with Peppers
Baked Potato
Stewed Pears   Cookies

Breakfast
Orange or Grapefruit Juice
Broiled Ham or Bacon
Corn Hoecake or Thin Toast
Strawberry Jam
Coffee or Milk

Lunch
Broiled Pompano
Baked Potato   Steamed Spinach
Stewed Tomatoes
Celery

Dinner
(Vegetable Plate)
Boiled Cabbage with Ham Hock
Chow-Chow
Sweet Potato, baked half shell
Baked Pears   Cookies

Breakfast
Fresh Figs with Cream
Muffins   Bacon

Lunch
Wilted Endive with Bacon Dressing
Steamed Egg   Corn Sticks
Pineapple-Carrot-Raisin Pie

Dinner
Broiled Spanish Mackerel
with Lime Juice
Baked Potato   Celery
Pomegranate Sherbet
or
Sour-sop Sherbet

Breakfast
Silver Nip
(Grapefruit Juice Set in Ice)
Toast   Stewed Guavas
Milk or Coffee

Lunch
Oyster Stew
Celery   Sliced Tomato
Cocoanut Pie

Dinner
Pineapple-Orange Salad
Cream Chicken with Green Peas
Hot Biscuit   Roselle Jelly

Breakfast
Grapes
Waffles   Tupelo Honey

Lunch
Creamed Shrimp
Celery   Bread and Butter
Lemonade

Dinner
Melon-Peach Cocktail
Broiled Chicken   Haw Jelly
Broccoli   Carrots
Hot Biscuits

Breakfast
Papaya with Lime
Soft-cooked Eggs
Graham Toast   Milk

Lunch
Lettuce and Tomato Salad
Bread and Butter
Banana Sauce

Dinner
Cream Vegetable Soup
Meat   Steamed Chard
Creamed Potatoes
Graham Crackers

Breakfast
Baked Tomato
Bacon   Toast
Orange Marmalade

Lunch
Bean Soup   Graham Crackers
Milk   Pineapple Pie

Dinner
Cabbage-Pimento Salad
Fish Chowder   Baked Potato
Strawberry Shortcake

Breakfast
Sliced Figs and Cream
Scrambled Eggs
Baking Powder Biscuits

Lunch
Cottage Cheese Salad   Lettuce
Graham Muffins   Marmalade

Dinner
Fruit Cocktail
Baked Red Snapper   Creamed Carrots
Chinese Cabbage   Mango Sauce
Cookies

Breakfast
Glass of Florida Orange Juice
Poached Egg on Toast
Pineapple Jam

Lunch
Spinach with Egg
Graham Bread and Butter
Baked Banana

Dinner
Shrimp Salad   Tomato Sliced
Lady Peas   Summer Squash
Peanut Cookies   Fruit Juice

Breakfast
Rhubarb Sauce
Steamed Egg
Graham Toast   Butter

Lunch
Escalloped Potatoes
Stuffed Green Peppers
Cake   Glass of Milk

Dinner
Head Lettuce with
Thousand Island Dressing
Spiced Melon Pickle
Boiled Ham   Brown Bread
Cream Spinach   Baked Beans

Breakfast
Strawberries and Cream
Bacon   Waffles

Lunch
Oyster Omelet with Celery
Beets
Hot Baking Powder Biscuits
Pineapple Marmalade

Dinner
Roast Chicken
Green Peas   Mashed Potatoes
Tomato and Lettuce Salad
Cocoanut Cream Pie

Breakfast
Grapefruit
Bacon
Banana Sauce
Muffins   Milk

Lunch
Buttered Beets   Corn on the Cob
Hot Rolls, Buttered
Stewed Guavas

Dinner
Fruit Cup
Broiled Steak
Steamed Onion   Baked Potatoes
Sliced Tomato
Mango Brown Betty

NOTE—Milk has been mentioned only occasionally. Menus for children should be built around a quart of milk daily. Menus for grown-ups should include milk every day, the amount varying with the amount of vegetables and fruit used.

U. S. D. A. Issues Bulletins on Value of Vegetables in Diet

LIBERAL DIET

The liberal diet, as its name implies, provides very generously for all of the food requirements. It contains an abundance of fruits and vegetables, lean meats and eggs, as well as a generous allowance of milk. The liberal diet allows for better-than-average nutrition, because it provides more than amply for the items necessary for growth, health, and general well-being. It supplies in the course of the day or the week the following amounts of different foods, per person:

MILK: 1 quart daily for each child, 1 pint for each adult (to drink or in cooked food).
VEGETABLES AND FRUITS (some raw): 6 to 7 servings per person daily.
    1 serving daily of potatoes or sweet potatoes.
    1 serving daily of tomatoes or citrus fruit.
    9 to 10 servings a week of leafy, green, or yellow vegetables (once a day, sometimes twice).
    9 to 10 servings a week of other vegetables or of leafy, green, and yellow kinds.
    9 to 10 servings a week of fruit.
EGGS: 4 to 6 times a week; also some in cooking.
MEAT, FISH, OR POULTRY: Once a day, sometimes twice.
BREAD, BUTTER, CEREALS, AND DESSERTS: As desired, so long as they do not displace the protective foods.

This diet need not be made up of an expensive assortment of foods. With wise marketing and no food luxuries, this diet could be purchased September 10, 1935, for about $8.70 a week or $450 a year for a family of two. For a family of four (two moderately active adults, boy 10 and girl 8), this diet was approximately $15.80 a week or $820 a year; for about $28.00 a week or $1,450 a year for a family of seven (consisting of two moderately active adults, girl 15, boy 13, boy 10, girl 8, and child 3).

MODERATE-COST ADEQUATE DIET

The moderate-cost adequate diet is well described by its name. For a reasonable amount of money it provides all of the different nutrients in sufficient quantities to keep adults and children in good nutritional condition, with a surplus for safety. It contains a generous amount of milk and plenty of vegetables, fruits, eggs, and lean meat so that it allows for considerable variety from meal to meal and from day to day, as the following list shows:

MILK: 1 quart daily for each child, 1 pint for each adult (to drink or in cooked food).
VEGETABLES AND FRUITS (some raw): 4½ to 5 servings per person daily.
    1 serving daily of potatoes or sweet potatoes.
    1 serving daily of tomatoes or citrus fruits.
    1 serving daily of leafy, green, or yellow vegetables.
    3 to 5 servings a week of other vegetables.
    1 serving daily of fruit.
EGGS: 2 to 3 times a week for adults; 4 to 5 times for young children; a few in cooking.
MEAT, FISH, OR POULTRY: About 5 times a week. (Once a day if the meat dish is sometimes a meat and cereal combination so that the weekly meat allowance is not exceeded.)
A CEREAL dish daily.
BREAD AND BUTTER at every meal.
DESSERT once a day, sometimes twice, if desired.

The cost, about $6.50 a week or $335 a year for a family of two at prices as of September 10, 1935, is well within the reach of many families in this country. For a family of four (two moderately active adults, boy 10 and girl 8), the cost of this diet was about $12.40 a week or $640 a year; for a family of seven (two moderately active adults, girl 15, boy 13, boy 10, girl 8, and child 3), about $21.25 a week or $1,100 a year.

MINIMUM-COST ADEQUATE DIET

The minimum-cost adequate diet is the cheapest combination of foods that it is desirable to use for an indefinite period of time. In order to meet all nutritional needs as cheaply as possible, this diet has a large quantity of cereal products and milk as its basis. Just enough of vegetables, fruits, eggs, and lean meats are used to supply vitamins, minerals, and protein not adequately furnished by bread and milk, and enough of fats and sweets are included to round out the calories. The choice among the different kinds of foods is considerably limited by cost, and careful selection among the most nutritious of the less expensive kinds is essential. The list which follows indicates the number of servings of different foods per person for the day or the week:

MILK: 1 quart daily for each young child, ¾ of a quart daily for each child over four, 1 pint for each adult (to drink or in cooked food).

VEGETABLES AND FRUITS (some raw): From 3 to 4 servings per person daily.

    8 to 9 servings a week of potatoes and sweet potatoes (once a day, sometimes twice).

    2 to 3 servings a week of tomatoes (or of citrus fruits in season) for each adult and child over four; 4 tablespoons of tomato juice or 2 tablespoons of orange juice daily for each child under four.

    5 to 6 servings a week of leafy, green, or yellow vegetables.

    2 to 3 servings a week of dried beans, peas, or peanuts.

    1 serving daily of fruit or an additional vegetable (including some leafy, green or yellow kinds).

EGGS: 2 to 3 times a week for adults; 4 to 5 times for young children; a few in cooking.

MEAT OR FISH: 3 to 4 times a week (more frequently if the meat dish is often a meat and cereal combination so that the weekly meat allowance is not exceeded).

A CEREAL dish once a day, sometimes twice.

BREAD at every meal; BUTTER at some meals.

DESSERTS about once a day if desired; cereal pudding, cookies, simple cake, short-cake, and inexpensive pastries and fruits are suitable.

    This diet could be purchased September 10, 1935, for about $4.85 a week or $250 a year for two moderately active adults; for about $9.15 a week or $475 a year for a family of four (two moderately active adults, boy 10 and girl 8); for about $15.60 a week or $810 a year for a family of seven (two moderately active adults, girl 15, boy 13, boy 10, girl 8, and child 3).

RESTRICTED DIET

    The restricted diet plan is suggested only for emergency use, because it may not provide a sufficient surplus of protective foods (milk, eggs, citrus fruits, and green vegetables) to insure good health over an indefinite period of time. Because of the very limited quantity of the protective foods it contains, very wise choice from among the cheapest most nutritious foods must be made for this diet. Even with its shortcomings, it is a better diet for the amount of money it costs than would be obtained by choosing foods at random, and it does allow for some variety, as the following list shows:

MILK: 1 pint daily for each child. 1 cup for each adult, to drink or in cooked food.

VEGETABLES AND FRUITS (some raw): About 2½ to 3 servings daily.

    8 to 9 servings a week of potatoes and sweet potatoes (once a day, sometimes twice).

    2 to 3 servings a week of tomatoes (or of citrus fruits in season), for each adult and child over four; 4 tablespoons of tomato juice or 2 tablespoons of orange juice daily for each child under four.

    3 small servings a week of leafy, green, or yellow vegetables.

    2 to 3 servings a week of dried beans, peas, or peanuts.

    3 to 4 small servings a week of other vegetables or fruits.

EGGS: Once a week for adults, twice for children under four.

MEAT OR FISH: 2 servings a week (more frequently if the meat dish is often a meat and cereal combination so that the weekly meat allowance is not exceeded).

A CEREAL dish at least once a day, usually twice.

BREAD in some form at every meal, butter at some meals.

DESSERT occasionally; cereal pudding, gingerbread, or one-egg cake, and dried fruits or other inexpensive kinds are suitable.

    This diet could be purchased September 10, 1935, for about $3.25 a week or $170 a year for two moderately active adults; for about $6.10 a week or $320 a year for a family of four (two moderately active adults, boy 10 and girl 8); for about $10.50 a week or $545 a year for a family of seven (two moderately active adults, girl 15, boy 13, boy 10, girl 8, and child 3).

VII—Tables

1. CALORY TABLE

(Selected from "Feeding the Family"—Mary Swartz Rose, and from Bulletin 28, U. S. Department of Agriculture.)

Select 600 out of 3000 calories daily from fruits and vegetables. The following table is for convenience in planning menus. The number of calories for ordinary servings rather than the usual 100-calory portion is given.

Serving	C.	Serving	C.
Asparagus (5 tips)	25	Tomatoes (1 cup cream soup)	125
Celery (1 cup, chopped)	15	Bananas (average size)	125
Cauliflower (4 heaping tablespoons)	20	Blackberries (3 heaping tablesps.)	60
Cabbage (1 cup, shredded)	20	Cantaloupe (½ melon)	90
Carrots (1 medium)	100	Grapefruit (½ large)	140
Corn (1 medium ear)	100	Grapes (1 large bunch)	110
Brussels sprouts (four)	50	Blueberries (4 heaping tablespoons)	80
Beets (2 heaping tablespoons)	30	Orange (average)	100
Beans (string, ½ cup)	25	Peach (average)	45
Beans (limas, fresh, 2 tablespoons)	100	Pear (average)	90
Eggplant (¼ medium)	50	Pineapple (2 slices)	45
Lemons (1 large)	30	Plum (average)	25
Lettuce (½ head)	25	Strawberries (4 heaping tablesps.)	40
Onions (½ medium)	25	Watermelon (large slice)	40
Parsnips (medium)	75	Marmalade (orange), 1 tablesp.	100
Potato (medium white, baked)	100	Butter, 1 tablespoon	100
Potato (medium sweet, baked)	150	Milk (whole, 1 glass)	170
Peas (green), ½ cup	75	Egg (1 medium)	75
Peas (field), ½ cup	100	Cheese (1⅛ inch cube)	100
Strawberries (1 cup)	35	Bread (2½ inch slices, white)	100
Squash (2 heaping tablespoons)	70	Corn muffins (1 medium)	125
Spinach (2 heaping tablespoons)	60	Molasses (1½ tablespoons)	100
Turnip (2 heaping tablespoons)	15	Sugar (2 tablespoons)	100
Tomatoes (medium), uncooked	40	Cream (thin, ¼ cup)	100
Tomatoes (stewed, ½ cup)	25	Wesson Oil (1 tablespoon)	100

2. VITAMIN TABLE

Reported occurrence of vitamins A, B, and C in fruits and vegetables.
Selected from Circular 84, U. S. Department of Agriculture.
Sibyl L. Smith, Senior Chemist. Experiment Station.
‡ indicates that the food contains the vitamin.
‡ ‡ indicates that the food is a good source of the vitamin.
‡ ‡ ‡ indicates that the food is an excellent source of the vitamin.
— indicates that the food contains no appreciable amount of the vitamin.
* indicates that evidence is lacking or appears insufficient.

Relative distribution of vitamins A, B, and C

FRUITS AND VEGETABLES

ITEM	A	B	C
Fruits:			
Avocados	‡ ‡ ‡ ‡	‡ ‡ ‡ ‡	*
Bananas, baked in skin	*	*	‡ ‡ ‡ ‡
Bananas, baked without skin	*	*	‡ ‡
Bananas, raw	‡ to ‡ ‡	‡	‡ ‡ ‡ ‡
Breadfruit	‡ ‡ ‡ ‡	*	*
Cactus (pricklypear)	*	*	‡ ‡ ‡ ‡

VITAMIN TABLE—(Continued)

Relative distribution of vitamins A, B, and C

FRUITS AND VEGETABLES

ITEM	A	B	C
Fruits—Continued:			
Cantaloupes	+ + + +	+ + + +	+ + + +
Cashew apples	+ +	*	*
Chicos (sapodillas)	+ + + +	*	+ + + +
Custard apples	—	*	*
Grapefruit (or juice), fresh	+ +	+ +	+ + +
Grapefruit juice, dried	*	+ +	+ + +
Grapefruit peel, outer	— to +	+ +	*
Grape juice, dried	*	*	—
Grapes (or juice), fresh	+	+ to + +	+
Guavas	*	*	+ +
Lemon juice, concentrated	*	*	+ + +
Lemon juice, dried	*	+ +	+ + +
Lemon juice, frozen, stored	*	*	+
Lemon peel, outer	+	+ +	—
Lemons, cold storage	*	*	+ + +
Lemons (or juice), fresh	+	+ +	+ + +
Lime juice, concentrated	*	*	+ +
Limes (or juice)	—	*	+ +
Mangoes, dried	*	*	+
Mangoes, ripe and unripe	+	*	*
Mulberries	*	*	+
Orange juice, concentrated	+ +	*	+ + +
Orange juice, dried	+ +	+ +	+ + +
Orange juice, fresh	+ +	+ +	+ + +
Orange juice, frozen, stored	*	*	+
Orange peel, dried and fresh	*	*	+ +
Orange peel, inner	*	+	*
Orange peel, outer	+ +	+	+ +
Oranges, cold storage	*	*	+ + +
Papaya juice	*	*	+ + +
Papayas	+ +	+	+ + +
Peaches, canned	+ to + +	+	+ to + +
Peaches, cooked	*	*	+
Peaches, dried	*	*	+
Peaches, raw	+ to + +	+	+ +
Pears, canned (cold-packed)	*	*	— to +
Pears, cooked	*	*	—
Pears, raw, fresh	*	+ to + +	+
Pears, raw, stored	*	*	+

VITAMIN TABLE—(Continued)

Relative distribution of vitamins A, B, and C

FRUITS AND VEGETABLES

ITEM	A	B	C
Fruits—Continued:			
Pineapples, canned	‡ ‡	‡ ‡	‡ ‡
Pineapples, raw	+ +	+ +	‡ ‡
Plantains (baking bananas)	‡ ‡	‡ ‡	*
Strawberries, canned and raw	+	+	+ + +
Tamarind, dried	*	*	+
Tangerines	*	*	+ + +
Vegetables:			
Artichokes, globe	‡ ‡	+	*
Asparagus, bleached	—	*	*
Asparagus, green, canned	‡ ‡	*	*
Asparagus, green, cooked	‡ ‡	*	*
Asparagus, green, raw	‡ ‡	+ + +	*
Beets, leaves	‡ ‡	‡ ‡	*
Beets, roots	— to +	+	+
Beets, stems	*	+	*
Cabbage, Chinese	*	*	‡ ‡
Cabbage, head, canned	*	*	+
Cabbage, head, cooked	+	‡ ‡	+
Cabbage, head, raw	+	‡ ‡	+ + +
Cabbage, leaves, green, dried	‡ to ‡ ‡	‡ ‡	+
Cabbage, leaves, green, fresh	‡ ‡	‡ ‡	+ + +
Cabbage, leaves, green, stored	*	*	— to +
Cabbage, leaves, white, fresh	— to +	‡ ‡	+ + +
Carrots, autoclaved	+ + +	*	*
Carrots, canned, young	*	*	—
Carrots, cooked, old	*	‡ ‡	— to +
Carrots, cooked, young	*	‡ ‡	+
Carrots, raw, old	+ + +	‡ ‡	+
Carrots, raw, young	+ + +	‡ ‡	‡ ‡
Cauliflower, canned	*	*	—
Cauliflower, cooked	*	‡ to ‡ ‡	*
Cauliflower, raw	+	‡ ‡	+
Celery, leaves, bleached	+	*	*
Celery, leaves, green	‡ ‡	*	*
Celery, stalks, bleached	— to +	‡ ‡	*
Celery, stalks, ethylene bleached	*	‡ ‡	*
Chard, Swiss, autoclaved	‡ ‡	*	*
Chard, Swiss, raw	‡ ‡	‡ to ‡ ‡	*
Chayotes	‡ ‡	*	*

VITAMIN TABLE—(Continued)
Relative distribution of vitamins A, B, and C
FRUITS AND VEGETABLES

ITEM	A	B	C
Vegetables—Continued:			
Collards, cooked	+++ +++	+ +	+ +
Collards, raw	+++	++	++
Cowpeas, cooked	*	++ ++	*
Cowpeas, dried	++	*	*
Cowpeas, sprouted	*	*	+++
Cucumbers	— to +	+	++
Dasheens	+ + +	+ to ++	+ ++
Dasheens, steamed	+	+	+
Eggplant	+ +	+ +	*
Endive	+ +	*	+ +
Escarole	+++ +++	*	*
Kale	++ ++	*	*
Kohl-rabi	*	*	+ +
Lettuce, head	+ to ++	++	+++
Lettuce, leaves, bleached	+	++ ++	+++ +++
Lettuce, leaves, green	+++	++	+++
Okra	*	++ ++	*
Onions, cooked	— to +	+	+
Onions, raw	— to +	+	++
Parsley	*	++ ++	*
Parsnips	— to +	++ ++	*
Peas, dried	+	++ ++	*
Peas, green, canned	++	+ to ++	++
Peas, green, cooked	++	+ to ++	++
Peas, green, raw	++	++	+++
Peppers, green	++	++	+++
Poi (fermented, steamed, dasheens)	+	+	+
Potatoes, baked	+	++	+ to ++
Potatoes, boiled 15 minutes	+	++	++
Potatoes, boiled 1 hour	+	++	+
Potatoes, peel	*	+	*
Potatoes, peeled, boiled, and dried	*	+	*
Potatoes, raw	+	++	++
Pumpkins, boiled	++	*	*
Pumpkins, dried	+++	+	*
Pumpkins, raw	++	+	+

VITAMIN TABLE—(Continued)

Relative distribution of vitamins A, B, and C

FRUITS AND VEGETABLES

ITEM	A	B	C
Vegetables—Continued:			
Radishes	—	+ + + +	+ + + +
Rhubarb	*	*	+ +
Romaine	+ + + +	+ + + +	*
Rutabaga juice	*	*	+ + + + + +
Rutabaga juice, frozen, stored 15 months	*	*	— to +
Rutabaga juice, heated................	*	*	+ + + +
Rutabagas, cold storage...............	*	*	+ + + +
Rutabagas, raw (Swedes).............	+	+ + + +	+ + + + + +
Soybeans	+ +	+ + + +	—
Soybeans, sprouted	*	*	—
Spinach, canned	+ + + + + +	+ +	+ to + + + +
Spinach, cooked	+ + + + + +	+ +	+ to + + + +
Spinach, dried	+ + + + + +	+ + + +	*
Spinach, raw	+ + + + + +	+ + + +	+ + + + + +
Squash, Hubbard, autoclaved and raw..	+ + + +	*	*
Sweet potatoes, autoclaved............	+ to + + + +	*	*
Sweet potatoes, raw..................	+ to + + + +	+ +	+ +
Tomato, concentrate	+ + + + + +	+ + + + + +	+ + + + + +
Tomato juice, dried...................	*	+ + + +	+ + + +
Tomatoes, green, canned..............	*	*	+ +
Tomatoes, green, pickled..............	*	*	— to +
Tomatoes, green, raw, mature.........	+	+ + + +	+
Tomatoes, raw, air-ripened............	+ + + +	+ + + +	+ + + +
Tomatoes, raw, ethylene-ripened.......	+ + + +	+ + + +	+ + + +
Tomatoes, raw, vine-ripened...........	+ + + +	+ + + +	+ + + + + +
Tomatoes, ripe, canned...............	+ + + +	+ + + +	++ to +++
Turnip greens, cooked................	+ + + + + +	+ + + +	— to +
Turnip greens, raw...................	+ + + + + +	+ + + +	+ + + +
Turnips, white	— to +	+ + + +	+ + + +
Vegetable marrow, juice..............	*	*	+ + + +
Water Cress	+ + + + + +	*	+ + + + + +

VITAMINS—HELP YOURSELF

*(By Hazel E. Munsell, Bureau of Home Economics,
U. S. Department of Agriculture)*

Vitamins are important substances that are essential for good health, growth, vigor, and general well-being of the body. They are often described as necessary body regulators, since their function is to stimulate growth and protect health rather than to furnish the material for building tissue or supplying energy.

Foods that are rich in one or more vitamins are frequently called "protective foods."

Each of the six vitamins so far discovered is described below and a list of foods rich in each is given. These foods have been selected on the basis of experimental work done in many laboratories including the Nutrition Laboratory of the Bureau of Home Economics. All foods listed are known to be good sources.

Further experiments may make it possible to extend the lists to include other foods.

VITAMIN A

Vitamin A protects the body against a number of troublesome bacterial infections. It also stimulates growth and is necessary for well-being at all ages. Without a regular supply of vitamin A a person loses vitality and may develop infections in the eyes, sinuses, ears, glands of the mouth and throat, and in some instances in the kidneys and bladder. Foods having a yellow or green color are generally rich sources of this vitamin. Green leaves, yellow corn, and sweet potatoes, for instance, are better sources than bleached leaves, white corn, and white potatoes. Thin green leaves are very valuable for their vitamin A content.

Vitamin A is called the "fat soluble vitamin" because it is soluble in fats. It is only slightly soluble in water and is less affected by heat than some of the other vitamins.

GOOD SOURCES OF VITAMIN A—*Animal Products:* Cod-liver oil, butter, milk, salmon, liver, cream, egg yolk, cheese, whole milk, kidney.

Plant Products—Green and yellow vegetables: Spinach, escarole, romaine, green lettuce, kale, water cress, turnip tops, broccoli, endive, chard, collards, green cabbage, beet leaves, mustard, dandelion greens, brussels sprouts, snap beans, carrots, sweet potatoes, peas, yellow squash, peppers, asparagus, red and yellow tomatoes.

Fruits: Bananas, apricots, yellow peaches, muskmelon, plantain (baking banana), pineapple, papaya, oranges, prunes, watermelon.

VITAMIN B

Vitamin B is necessary for good appetite and also for normal muscle tone in the digestive tract. Loss of appetite and general listlessness, sluggish digestive systems, and nervous irritability result from a continued diet short in vitamin B, while an absolute lack of this vitamin brings on a muscular paralysis or the disease known as beriberi. Vitamin B is very important to the nursing mother and the baby. Without enough of it, the mother's milk may be poor in quality, and with still less of the vitamin, the mother may even fail to secrete milk. Plenty of vitamin B in the mother's diet also provides the infant with a sufficient supply of vitamin B.

The list of foods containing vitamin B is long, since a large number of foods contain a little. Whole seeds such as whole-grain cereals and nuts are valuable sources because vitamin B is concentrated in the germ portion. Many fruits and vegetables are also good sources.

Vitamin B is destroyed by heat more readily than vitamin A, and long cooking of vegetables is therefore undesirable. Also, since this vitamin is very soluble in water, it may be easily "washed out" in cooking when much water is used. An alkaline substance, like soda, greatly increases the amount of vitamin B destroyed. This is one reason why cooking green vegetables with soda to preserve the green color is a very bad practice.

GOOD SOURCES OF VITAMIN B—*Animal Products:* Milk, liver, kidney, heart, egg yolk, lean pork, brains, oysters.

Plant Products: Vegetables: broccoli, asparagus, spinach, tomatoes, peas, kale, snap beans, romaine, turnip greens, mustard greens, chard, celery, sweet potatoes, white potatoes, cabbage, collards, beet leaves, cauliflower, lettuce, okra, green peppers, carrots, onions, parsnips, rutabagas, turnips.

Fruits: Grapefruit, lemons, oranges, fresh and canned pineapple, bananas, apples, peaches, avocado, grapes, fresh prunes, dates, cherries.

Seeds: Whole grains—wheat, rye, corn, rice, barley, oats. Nuts—almonds, walnuts, chestnuts, brazil nuts, pecans, peanuts. Legumes—beans (all kinds), cowpeas, lentils, dried peas. Yeasts.

VITAMIN C

A daily supply of vitamin C is essential for children and adults. The necessity of having adequate amounts of vitamin C in the diet is stressed by all who recognize the importance of good "tooth nutrition." Bleeding gums, loose teeth, sore joints, loss of appetite with loss of weight and fatigue, are symptoms that develop when the diet is extremely low or lacking in vitamin C.

An acute condition of this kind has long been known as scurvy. Though scurvy is rare in this country, many borderline cases with such symptoms as sore gums, loose and decayed teeth, and "rheumatism" occur when the diet contains some vitamin C but not enough.

Vitamin C is easily destroyed by heat at fairly low temperatures and is most easily destroyed in an alkaline solution, such as water containing soda. Cooked foods cannot be depended upon entirely for vitamin C nor does the body store a supply of this vitamin, hence the need for some raw fruits and raw vegetables every day.

GOOD SOURCES OF VITAMIN C—*Fruits:* Oranges, grapefruit, lemons, tangerines, apples, strawberries, cranberries, bananas, peaches (fresh and canned), pineapple (fresh and canned), raspberries, watermelon, papaya, muskmelon, currants, gooseberries.

Vegetables: Cabbage, tomatoes (fresh and canned), spinach (fresh and canned), peas (fresh and canned), broccoli, rutabagas, collards, snap beans, endive, peppers, water cress, carrots, corn (fresh and canned), turnips, turnip greens, escarole, legumes (sprouted), rhubarb, white potatoes, sweet potatoes, cucumbers, cauliflower, onions, radishes, beets.

VITAMIN D

The mineral elements, calcium and phosphorus, are required in the building of teeth and bones, but unless vitamin D is present in the diet, these tissues will not develop normally, and stunted growth and rickets may result. There are only a few foods that contain vitamin D in large enough quantities to be considered good sources. A chemical substance, ergosterol, is changed into vitamin D by ultraviolet light. Foods containing this substance are often exposed to the rays of an ultraviolet lamp and thus enriched with vitamin D. The addition of irradiated ergosterol offers another means of supplying vitamin D to a food product.

Human skin contains a small quantity of ergosterol which may be changed into vitamin D by ultraviolet light. This explains how rickets may be prevented and cured by exposure of the skin to sunlight containing ultraviolet rays.

This vitamin is not easily destroyed by heat, so ordinary cooking does not affect it.

GOOD SOURCES OF VITAMIN D. Cod-liver oil.

Other foods that contain some vitamin D: Egg yolk, milk, butter, salmon, oysters, California sardines. Foods enriched with vitamin D by the Steenbock process of irradiation with ultraviolet light.

VITAMIN E

Vitamin E is essential for reproduction and is known as the antisterility vitamin. It occurs in a great many foods in small quantities but the germ of the wheat grain is especially rich. Vegetable oils, green lettuce, and a number of other vegetables contain considerable quantities of vitamin E. It is not easily destroyed by heat.

VITAMIN G

Vitamin G is essential for well-being at all ages and especially for preventing the appearance of premature old age. A continued deficiency of vitamin G causes slowing up of growth or loss of weight, sore mouth, digestive disturbances, and in time a sensitiveness and inflammation of the skin. These symptoms are very similar to those of pellagra, a disease common to certain sections of the South where families are known to live on an inadequate diet.

Foods that contain vitamin G are beneficial in preventing and curing pellagra. This vitamin occurs in many foods in moderate or small quantities. The best sources now known are yeast, lean meats, eggs, milk (either whole or skimmed, fresh, canned or dried), green leaves, and the germ portion of cereals.

Like vitamin B, vitamin G is very soluble in water. It withstands the heat of cooking much better than vitamin B, but is destroyed when soda or other alkaline substances are present.

GOOD SOURCES OF VITAMIN G—*Animal Products:* Whole milk (fresh, evaporated, dried), skim milk (fresh, dried), buttermilk, cheese, eggs, meat liver (beef and pork), kidney, spleen, heart, lean cuts of beef, pork or lamb, salmon.

Plant Products: Green leaves, mustard, turnip tops, kale, beet tops, carrot tops, collards, spinach, broccoli, water cress.

Fruits: Bananas.

Germ portion of cereals; wheat germ; yeast.

Reprinted from

THE JOURNAL of THE AMERICAN COLLEGE of PROCTOLOGY

448 South Hill Street, Los Angeles, California

Vitamins and Their Relations to Deficiency Diseases of the Alimentary Tract

EDWARD A. JOHNSTON, M.D., *Minneapolis, Minnesota*

In the consideration of rectal and intestinal troubles, using the simple words instead of the more scientific and possibly more elegant term, syndrome, which might be more fitting, we have observed throughout many years conditions of deficiencies of specific food substances. These deficiencies alter the normal metabolism.

The metabolism of the human body, being an animal function, is a breaking down precess of constructive metabolism of plant life. The animal or human body *cannot synthetize organic compounds from inorganic sources and is dependent, to a great extent, on vegetables for organic food.* Vitamins as catalysts are one of the most important of these food substances.

When we consider that vitamins in the food are the substances with which the endocrines are able to secrete their active principles, it is apparent that a glandular insufficiency may take place in the absence of vitamins. Vitamins are a class of organic compounds that are probably the most complex food constituents. All of the ductless glands, the thyroid, para-thyroid, thymus, pineal body, pituitary, adrenals, gonads, pancreas, islets of Langerhans, and spleen must have one or more of the vitamins in order to secrete their vital fluids, and, if deprived of the vitamins, will atrophy and cease to function.

It is difficult to give a definite evaluation of the role of single vitamins or specific food substances needed for normal metabolism. The evidence given by all investigators of vitamin deficiencies, point toward multiple deficiencies over a protracted period of time. The difference between enough and not enough in the earlier stages is not always apparent. These deficiencies occur despite a balanced diet, the balance of which is usually determined to a great extent by older knowledge of nutrition, and influenced by conditions in commercial preparation and preservation or cost beyond the control of the average person. We may further find that foods in certain areas are from a vitamin deficient belt just as we know of the iodine deficient belt in the Great Lakes basin today.

The action of vitamin A is principally upon the epithelial surfaces, the skin and mucous membrances, and in fact all of the lining surfaces from mouth to anus. Vitamin A protects us from infection at every point through which it might enter the body. Vitamin A deficiency, by its action of increasing epithelial infectivity and infectability, can be an important factor in the cause of ulcers. *Sure*, discussing the cause of stomach ulcers, says, "Deficiencies of Vitamins A, B and D, cause a progressive loss of power of the body surface to control the bacterial life in contact with it." Stomach ulcers are probably the best instance of bacterial invasion primarily due to a lowered resistance resulting from a vitamin deficiency. Other instances of vitamin A deficiency, and often found in conjunction with infections of the intestinal tract, are infections of the eyes, tonsils, sinuses, lungs, buccal and lingual mucosa, and the skin. In a history of a patient with colitis or ulcerations in any part of the intestinal or rectal tract, oral and skin lesions are often present and there is usually a picture of low plasma protein, inverted albumin-globulin ratio, low serum calcium and a total low base in the blood determination. *(Mackie.)*

Richards has shown that the earliest macroscopic signs of disease in vitamin A deficient rats are to be seen in the digestive tract. Inflammation of the small intestines and cecum is frequent and the glandular portion of the stomach shows pitting and ulcerations, the digestive lesions occurring after three or four weeks on a deficient diet. *Mackie* and *Pound* have corroborated this with X-ray evidence in the human subject. "When deficiencies are present in an advanced degree they have been invariably associated with characteristic changes in the small intestines." Other vitamins when deficient give indications similarly, attesting to the related and cooperative action.

Vitamin B deficiency can be considered an important factor in the cause of hemorrhoids. It is essential to the maintenance of tonicity of muscular tissue in general, and a deficiency results invariably in a dilation of vascular walls through the effect upon the muscular layer. This is borne out by *Etzel,* who states that "Megaesophagus and megacolon are two abnormalities that frequently co-exist with polyneuritis, disturbances of the gastric chemism (anachlorhydria and hypochlor-hydria), dyspahagia, and constipation. Changes in the electrocardiogram are also seen in beriberi, both in man and in animals. Megacolon was produced in animals with avitaminosis B."

We can therefore draw the conclusion that the enlarged flabby colon and esophagus are due to a deficiency of B by its resulting loss of muscle tonicity, partial failure of elimination, with obstipation as the end result. It is an established fact that vitamin B contributes to the nutrition of the pituitary. It is more than probable that both the vasopressin and oxytocin of the pituitary are produced in normal amounts where B is available. The deficiency of vasopressin plus the nerve malfunction attributable to B deficiency can easily be responsible for the venous dilation, relaxation and congestion that is necessary for the development of hemorrhoids. It is a universal characteristic of B deficiency that the vascular system becomes dilated and degenerated, smaller networks disappearing, large vessels becoming larger.

Vitamin C is essential to the health of the endothelium. This includes the intima of the blood vessels. *Takahashi* noted a pronounced lowering of resistance to bacterial infection in his animal experiments in B and C deficiencies. In C deficiency, capillary hemorrhages are characteristic. In fact, the use of the capillary strength as a test for C deficiency is at present recognized as a reliable method. This also contributes to the destruction of the small networks or plexuses. "Rats stunted by B deficiency have bone lesions that are identical with those in guinea pigs suffering from acute and uncomplicated scurvy, C deficiency. Marrow elements are destroyed and replaced by reticular tissue supporting widely dilated, congested blood vessels." *(Shipley, McCollum, and Simmonds.)* That reference demonstrates the co-operative action of vitamins B and C, both being essential to vascular health, degeneration occurring in the absence of either. Deficiency of vitamin B invariably results in relaxation of the muscular walls of the stomach or ptosis (one of the causes of loss of appetite), and enlargement in general of the intestinal tubes, with impairment of peristalsis. Less conspicuous, but no doubt no less consistent, is the vascular atony, and the slowing of the heart that has been suggested as a specific test for B deficiency *(Burch).* That is probably a consequence purely due to this dilation. It must be recalled that the pulse rate slows whenever an artery and vein are experimentally interconnected, to demonstrate the physiologic law that the heart tends to move a constant volume of blood, the pulse rate and pressure both rising against arterial construction and vice versa.

In vitamin D deficiency we note the low serum calcium. Dietary calcium is not absorbed and no calcium is made available in the serum calcium of the blood for the tissues. Glands supplying digestive fluids require considerable calcium according to *Clouse.* "Vitamin D might bring about increases in blood calcium and phosphorus either by increasing the excretion through the kidney or intestines or both." It is noticeable that nervousness and irritability are occasioned by low serum calcium.

Nervous imbalance and paralysis were noted by *Evans & Burr* in the absence of vitamin E. This is probably due to one of the actions of vitamin E concerned in mineral metabolism. Vitamin E promotes the supply of magnesium and calcium to the tissues. The mineral supply to the different organs are, no doubt, controlled by the different vitamins and by a process of biochemical affinity the organs select some specifically useful molecules, which brings to mind some of the points in the law of homeopathy. This mineral metabolism control of the vitamins may have some bearing on the report made recently by *Dr. Davidson* to the A. M. A. Convention, Atlantic City, where he gave evidence of cure of cancer induced by tar in rats, with the use of vitamin E. Magnesium deficiencies have been pointed out as a possible cause of cancer by some investigators, but it is more probable that vitamin E is of greater concern. Cancer having a particular affinity for the intestinal and rectal tract, may be caused by a systemic deficiency, lowering the resistance to a point where the degenerative process begins.

Little is known of vitamin F but it seems to be concerned with calcium metabolism. A dry skin and some anemias are thought to be caused by deficiencies of F.

It will be seen from the foregoing that vitamin deficiencies may be a factor worthy of consideration in infections, degenerations and malignancies. Therefore, when the conditions of deficiencies are recognized and local treatment is administered to the infected areas, the conditions bringing about the deficiencies should be adjusted. The diet should contain quantities of fresh vegetables, eaten as nearly in the natural state as possible and few refined foods should be allowed in the regimen. Concentrates of the vitamins are a valuable aid in correcting the acute stage in which the patient is found when symptoms develop. There are several good vitamin preparations on the market, but with the matter of economy as well as the fact most deficiencies that occur are multiple, rules out the use of the vitamins in a single concentrate. With the use of one single vitamin, some improvement will occur, but may then be arrested, and no further improvement will follow until the balance be established by administration of additional supporting vitamins. I have had very good results in a number of patients on a group vitamin concentrate tablet with all the vitamins present. This is effective and is not too expensive to the patient.

Much clinical and laboratory work has been done on vitamins, but much more remains to be done before we have a thorough picture of the part vitamins play in normal health. However, without newer knowledge of nutrition, our present knowledge of the effects of vitamin insufficiency, and the availability of some promising concentrates, we can proceed to effect a greater percentage of cures, than has heretofore been possible.

It behooves every medical man to study and observe the merits of vitamin therapy. Only superior knowledge of the worth and the use of this valuable addition to our armentarium will enable us to protect humanity from its indiscretions, especially by excessive vitamin self-medication.

FRUITS GROWN IN SOUTH FLORIDA

Avocado
Ambarella
Akee
Banana
Custard Apple
Canistel
Coco Plum
Citrus
Ceriman
Cereus (Pitayz)
Carob Plum
Cashew
Carissa
Carambola
Cacao
Fig
Granadilla

Grapes
Guava
Ilama
Jaboticaba
Jackfruit
Jujube
Ketembilla
Lichti
Loquat
Mamey
Mamoncill
Mango
Papaya
Para Guava
Peach
Persimmon (Japanese)
Pineapple

Pitaya
Pomegranate
Prickly Pear
Rhubarb
Rose Apple
Roselle
Sapodilla
Sapote
Seagrape
Sour Sop
Star Apple
Sugar Apple
Surinam Cherry
Tamarind
Umkokolo
Watermelon
White Sapote

VEGETABLES GROWN IN SOUTH FLORIDA

Beans (limas)
Beans (string)
Beets (roots)
Beets (greens)
Broccoli
Brussels Sprouts
Cabbage
Cabbage (Chinese)
Carrots
Cassava
Cauliflower
Chayote
Collards
Corn (sweet)

Cucumber
Dasheen
Eggplants
Endive
Escarole
Greens (turnips)
Kale
Kohl-Rabi
Lettuce
Mustard (greens)
Mustard (Chinese)
Parsley
Peas (English, field, pigeon)
Pepper (sweet)

Pepper (red)
Potato (white, sweet, yam)
Okra
Onion
Rape
Radish
Rutabaga
Spinach
Squash (Chinese)
Squash
Swiss Chard
Turnips (roots)
Tomatoes
Water Cress

4. WEIGHT-HEIGHT-AGE TABLES

WEIGHT-HEIGHT-AGE TABLES FOR GIRLS—From Birth to School Age.*

Height inches	1 mo.	3 mos.	6 mos.	9 mos.	12 mos.	18 mos.	24 mos.	30 mos.	36 mos.	48 mos.	60 mos.	72 mos.
20	8											
21	9	10										
22	10	11										
23	11	12	13									
24	12	13	14	14								
25	13	14	15	15								
26		15	16	17	17							
27		16	17	18	18							
28			19	19	19	19						
29			19	20	20							
30				21	21	21	21					
31				22	22	23	23	23				
32					23	24	24	24	25			
33						25	25	25	26			
34						26	26	26	27			
35						29	29	29	29	29		
36								30	30	30	31	
37								31	31	31	32	
38									33	33	33	
39									34	34	34	34
40									35	36	36	36
41										37	37	37
42										39	39	39
43										40	41	41
44											42	42
45												45
46												47
47												50
48												52

*Prepared by Robert M. Woodbury, Ph.D.
Children's Bureau, U. S. Department of Labor.
Weight is stated to the nearest pound; height to the nearest inch; age to the nearest month.
Weight of children under 35 inches was taken without clothing; those of children above 35 inches with clothing (shoes, coat and sweater removed).
Published by
AMERICAN CHILD HEALTH ASSOCIATION, 370 Seventh Avenue, New York City.

WEIGHT-HEIGHT-AGE TABLES FOR BOYS—From Birth to School Age.*

Height inches	1 mo.	3 mos.	6 mos.	9 mos.	12 mos.	18 mos.	24 mos.	30 mos.	36 mos.	48 mos.	60 mos.	72 mos.
20	8											
21	9	10										
22	10	11										
23	11	12	13									
24	12	13	14									
25	13	14	15	16								
26		15	17	17	18							
27		16	18	18	19							
28			19	19	20	20						
29			20	20	21	21						
30					22	22	22	22				
31						23	23	23	24			
32						24	24	25	25			
33							26	26	26	27		
34							27	27	27	27		
35							29	29	29	29		
36								30	31	31	31	
37								32	32	32	32	
38									33	33	33	
39									35	35	35	
40									36	36	36	36
41										38	38	38
42										39	39	39
43										41	41	41
44											43	43
45											45	45
46												48
47												50
48												52
49												55

*Prepared by Robert M. Woodbury, Ph.D.
Children's Bureau, U. S. Department of Labor.

Weighing children is a means of ascertaining their rate of growth. All children should make a regular annual gain. These tables should be used as a means of interesting parents in their children's growth.

Lay infant on table on which has been placed an accurate measure. Stand child with heels and shoulders against a wall upon which has been marked or pasted an accurate measure.

Encourage the annual physical examination of every child by a physician.

WEIGHT-HEIGHT-AGE TABLES FOR GIRLS OF SCHOOL AGE†

Height (inches)	Average weight for height (lbs.)	5 yrs.	6 yrs.	7 yrs.	8 yrs.	9 yrs.	10 yrs.	11 yrs.	12 yrs.	13 yrs.	14 yrs.	15 yrs.	16 yrs.	17 yrs.	18 yrs.	19 yrs.
38	33	33	33													
39	34	34	34													
40	36	36	36	36*												
41	37	37	37	37*												
42	39	39	39	39*												
43	41	41	41	41	41*											
44	42	42	42	42	42*											
45	45	45	45	45	45	45*										
46	47	47*	47	47	48	48*										
47	50	49*	50	50	50	50	50*									
48	52			52	52	52	53*	53*								
49	55			54	55	55	56	56*								
50	58			56*	56	57	58	59	61	62*						
51	61				59	60	61	61	63	65						
52	64				63*	64	64	64	65	67						
53	68				66*	67	67	68	69	69	71*					
54	71					69	70	70	71	71	73*					
55	75				72*	74	74	74	75	77	78*					
56	79					76	78	78	79	81	83*					
57	84					80*	82	82	82	84	88	92*				
58	89						84	86	86	88	93	96*	101*			
59	95						87	90	90	92	96	100	103*	104*		
60	101						91*	95	95	97	101	105	108	109	111*	
61	108							99	100	101	105	108	112	113	116	
62	114							104*	105	106	109	113	115	117	118	
63	118								110	110	112	116	117	119	120	
64	121								114*	115	117	119	120	122	123	
65	125								118*	120	121	122	123	125	126	
66	129									124	124	125	128	129	130	
67	133									128*	130	131	133	133	135	
68	138									131*	133	135	136	138	138	
69	142										135*	137*	138*	140*	142*	
70	144										136*	138*	140*	142*	144*	
71	145										138*	140*	142*	144*	145*	

Age-Years	6	7	8	9	10	11	12	13	14	15	16	17	18
Av. height (inches):													
Short	43	45	47	49	50	52	54	57	59	60	61	61	61
Medium	45	47	50	52	54	56	58	60	62	63	64	64	64
Tall	47	50	53	55	57	59	62	64	66	66	67	67	67
Av. annual gain (lbs.):													
Short	4	4	4	5	6	6	10	13	10	7	2	1	
Medium	5	5	6	7	8	10	13	10	6	4	3	1	
Tall	6	8	8	9	11	13	9	8	4	4	1	1	

* NOTE—In order to extend the range of the tables so as to include weights of children who are taller or shorter than those in these groups there have been added as marked figures estimated weights. All the other weights represent averages for each inch in height and age of the children observed in this study.

† Prepared by Bird T. Baldwin, Ph.D., Iowa Child Welfare Research Station, State University of Iowa, and Thomas D. Wood, M.D., Columbia University, New York City.

WEIGHT-HEIGHT-AGE TABLE FOR BOYS OF SCHOOL AGE†

Height (inches)	Average weight for height (lbs.)	5 yrs.	6 yrs.	7 yrs.	8 yrs.	9 yrs.	10 yrs.	11 yrs.	12 yrs.	13 yrs.	14 yrs.	15 yrs.	16 yrs.	17 yrs.	18 yrs.	19 yrs.
38	34	34	34*													
39	35	35	35													
40	36	36	36*													
41	38	38	38	38*												
42	39	39	39	39	39*	39*										
43	41	41	41	41*												
44	44	44	44	44	44*											
45	46	46	46	46	46*	46*										
46	48	47*	48	48	48	48*										
47	50	49*	50	50	50	50*	50*									
48	53		52	53	53	53*										
49	55		55	55	55	55	55*									
50	58		57*	58	58	58	58	58*	58*							
51	61			61	61	61	61	61	61*							
52	64			63	64	64	64	64	64	64*						
53	68			66*	67	67	67	67	68	68*						
54	71				70	70	70	71	71	72*						
55	74				72*	72	73	73	74	74	74*	80*				
56	78				75*	76	77	77	78	78	78	83*				
57	82					79*	80	81	81	82	83	87				
58	85					83*	84	84	85	85	86	87				
59	89							87	88	89	89	90				
60	94						91*	92	92	93	94	95	96	106*		
61	99							95	96	97	99	100	103	107	111	
62	104							100*	101	102	103	104	107	111	116*	
63	111							105*	106	107	108	110	113	118	123	127*
64	117								109	111	113	115	117	121	126	130*
65	123								114*	117	118	120	122	127	131	134
66	129									119	122	125	128	132	136	139
67	133									124*	128	130	134	136	139	142
68	139										134	134	137	141	143	147
69	144										137	139	143	146	149	152
70	147										143	144	145	148	151	155
71	152										148*	150	151	152	154	159
72	157											153	155	156	158	163
73	163											157*	160	162	164	167
74	169											160*	164	168	170	171

Age-years	6	7	8	9	10	11	12	13	14	15	16	17	18	19
Av. Height (inches):														
Short	43	45	47	49	51	53	54	56	58	60	62	64	65	65
Medium	46	48	50	52	54	56	58	60	63	65	67	68	69	69
Tall	49	51	53	55	57	59	61	64	67	70	72	72	73	73
Av. annual gain (lbs.):														
Short	3	4	5	5	5	4	8	9	11	11	13	7	3	3
Medium	4	5	6	6	6	7	9	11	15	11	8	4	3	4
Tall	5	7	7	7	7	8	12	16	11	9	7	3	4	

* NOTE—In order to extend the range of the tables so as to include weights of children who are taller or shorter than those in these groups there have been added as marked figures estimated weights. All the other weights represent averages for each inch in height and age of the children observed in this study.

† Prepared by Bird T. Baldwin, Ph.D., Iowa Child Welfare Research Station, State University of Iowa, and Thomas D. Wood, M.D., Columbia University, New York City.

TABLE OF AVERAGE HEIGHTS AND WEIGHTS—MEN

AGE	5 ft. 0 in.	5 ft. 1 in.	5 ft. 2 in.	5 ft. 3 in.	5 ft. 4 in.	5 ft. 5 in.	5 ft. 6 in.	5 ft. 7 in.	5 ft. 8 in.	5 ft. 9 in.	5 ft. 10 in.	5 ft. 11 in.	6 ft. 0 in.	6 ft. 1 in.	6 ft. 2 in.	6 ft. 3 in.	6 ft. 4 in.	6 ft. 5 in.
15	107	109	112	115	118	122	126	130	134	138	142	147	152	157	162	167	172	177
20	117	119	122	125	128	132	136	140	144	148	152	156	161	166	171	176	181	188
25	122	124	126	129	133	137	141	145	149	153	157	162	167	173	179	184	189	194
30	126	128	130	133	136	140	144	148	152	156	161	166	172	178	184	190	196	201
35	128	130	132	135	138	142	146	150	155	160	165	170	176	182	189	195	201	207
40	131	133	135	138	141	145	149	153	158	163	168	174	180	186	193	200	206	212
45	133	135	137	140	143	147	151	155	160	165	170	176	182	188	195	202	209	215
50	134	136	138	141	144	148	152	156	161	166	171	177	183	190	197	204	211	217
55	135	137	139	142	145	149	153	158	163	168	173	178	184	191	198	205	212	219

TABLE OF AVERAGE HEIGHTS AND WEIGHTS—WOMEN

AGE	4 ft. 8 in.	4 ft. 9 in.	4 ft. 10 in.	4 ft. 11 in.	5 ft. 0 in.	5 ft. 1 in.	5 ft. 2 in.	5 ft. 3 in.	5 ft. 4 in.	5 ft. 5 in.	5 ft. 6 in.	5 ft. 7 in.	5 ft. 8 in.	5 ft. 9 in.	5 ft. 10 in.	5 ft. 11 in.	6 ft. 0 in.
15	101	103	105	106	107	109	112	115	118	122	126	130	134	138	142	147	152
20	106	108	110	112	114	116	119	122	125	128	132	136	140	143	147	151	156
25	109	111	113	115	117	119	121	124	128	131	135	139	143	147	151	154	158
30	112	114	116	118	120	122	124	127	131	134	138	142	146	150	154	157	161
35	115	117	119	121	123	125	127	130	134	138	142	146	150	154	157	160	163
40	119	121	123	125	127	129	132	135	138	142	146	150	154	158	161	164	167
45	122	124	126	128	130	132	135	138	141	145	149	153	157	161	164	168	171
50	125	127	129	131	133	135	138	141	144	148	152	156	161	165	169	173	176
55	125	127	129	131	133	135	138	141	144	148	153	158	163	167	171	174	177

Height and weight taken with shoes on and coat and vest or waist off.

Prepared by LIFE EXTENSION INSTITUTE.

INDEX